BEST of the BEST from SOUTH TEXAS AT&T PIONEERS COOKBOOK

Selected Recipes from
the Classic Pioneer Cookbooks

BEST of the BEST from SOUTH TEXAS AT&T PIONEERS COOKBOOK

Selected Recipes from
the Classic Pioneer Cookbooks

COMPILED BY
AT&T Pioneers of South Texas

PUBLISHED BY
QUAIL RIDGE PRESS
Preserving America's Food Heritage

Library of Congress Cataloging-in-Publication Data

Best of the best from South Texas AT & T Pioneers cookbook : selected recipes from the classic pioneer cookbooks / compiled by AT&T Pioneers of South Texas.
p. cm. — (Best of the best telephone pioneer cookbook series)
Includes index.
ISBN-13: 978-1-934193-49-5
ISBN-10: 1-934193-49-6
1. Cooking, American—Southern style. 2. Cooking—Texas, South. I. South Texas AT & T Pioneers.
TX715.2.S68B475 2010
641.59764--dc22 2010033648

ISBN-13: 978-1-934193-49-5 • ISBN-10: 1-934193-49-6

First printing, November 2010
Printed by Tara TPS in South Korea

Cover photo by Greg Campbell

On the cover: Ranch Hand Mexican Pie, page 138

QUAIL RIDGE PRESS
P. O. Box 123 • Brandon, MS 39043 • 1-800-343-1583
email: info@quailridge.com • www.quailridge.com

Contents

Pioneering in South Texas

Pioneers is the world's largest corporate volunteer organization. Founded in 1911 as the Telephone Pioneers of America, we're now more than 620,000 members strong—men and women committed to serving our communities in the United States, Canada, and beyond.

Pioneers is a network of volunteers who effect immediate, tangible change in local communities, in partnership with their sponsors. For a century, the Pioneers volunteer network has logged hundreds of millions of hours meeting specific needs in local communities.

Whether it's a cash donation to support a homeless shelter, or a one-on-one tutoring project to battle illiteracy, Pioneers make it possible for sponsor companies to get involved with communities they are in—giving back to their customer base, while building their pool of potential employees.

The South Texas Chapter consists of more than 20,000 dedicated men and women who come together as a team to "Improve the Quality of Life in our Communities." Our Regular Members, Life Members, and Pioneer Partners exemplify people caring about people throughout south Texas

For more information on the South Texas Pioneers, please visit www.attpioneervolunteers.org/SouthTexasTX64/HomeTX64.html.

at&t | pioneers
a volunteer network

Preface

When Southwestern Bell's acquisition of AT&T became official on November 18, 2005, it combined two outstanding telecommunications organizations that promised a new era of communications and entertainment for millions of people around the globe. This union not only merged our two businesses, it also merged our great volunteer organizations—The AT&T Pioneers.

You will find some fantastic recipes with this merging of several cookbooks from Pioneers throughout south Texas with the creation of the *Best of the Best from South Texas Pioneers Cookbook: Selected Recipes from the Classic Pioneers Cookbooks.*

Customers have praised the recipes found in all of the cookbooks. In fact, people have enjoyed the meals prepared using these cookbooks so much the requests for a book that combines the "Best of the Best" recipes has been a constant refrain from many of these cooks. Especially since all original cookbooks are out of print, this book brings the best of them back by popular demand. Now Pioneers from across the state of Texas have submitted their selections of time-tested and proven recipes from previous books such as *Country Favorites, Recipes to Remember,* and *Our Favorite Recipes*. These selections were compiled, sorted, and edited, and now grace the pages of this cookbook as a collection of the best recipes.

This compilation is possible due to the countless hours of work by many active and retired Pioneers over the years. We dedicate this cookbook to the thousands of volunteers who make up the AT&T Family and have shared their recipes. We hope that you enjoy them as much as our members have. Thank you for your support. Our pro-

Preface

ceeds will be used to support the various organizations in our Texas communities.

We expect this book to be the next essential cookbook for every household.

Joyce Earnest, 2010 President
South Texas Chapter #64– AT&T Pioneers

COOKBOOK COMMITTEE MEMBERS:
Jimmie Sue Lillie
Keith Pounds

Note from the Publisher

Quail Ridge Press was honored to be able to participate in the development and publication of the *Best of the Best from South Texas AT&T Pioneers Cookbook.*

The down-home, family-favorites in the South Texas Pioneers cookbooks are exactly the kind of recipes we seek to preserve—recipes that have been developed and perfected over generations; recipes that are legendary within a family and are now being shared with other families.

Each South Texas Pioneers cookbook has been reprinted many times. The cookbooks continue to be popular with young cooks as well as longtime cooks.

The AT&T Pioneers of South Texas, the organization of employees, retirees, and families of the telecommunications industry in Texas, are the force that have made the South Texas Pioneers cookbooks the success they are. The Pioneers are all volunteers who have given their time and energy to a variety of projects and activities that enrich our community.

I speak for all of us at Quail Ridge Press in saying that we are proud to be a part of this new cookbook that offers the finest recipes from the SOUTH TEXAS PIONEERS COOKBOOK SERIES. This new cookbook will continue to provide the Pioneers with the revenue that finances their worthy projects and will enable Quail Ridge Press to continue our goal of Preserving America's Food Heritage.

Gwen McKee, President
Quail Ridge Press
Brandon, Mississippi

Contributing Cookbooks

Cookins for Gulf Council

Published in 1982, and known as the "blue" cookbook, this collection of recipes gathered by the Gulf Coast Council of Pioneers and friends brings the best of south Texas cooking to the forefront.

Cookins for Gulf Coast Council II

The second cookbook from the Gulf Coast Council, known as the "red" cookbook, was published in 1985. All recipes were donated by telephone pioneers and friends working to make this a tried-and-true collection of Texas recipes to treasure for many generations.

Country Favorites

This collection of recipes from the Nacogdoches area of south Texas was published in 1994 by Telephone Pioneers of America Lake Country Club #57. The money raised from the sale of this book went to help the handicapped as well as many other service projects in the communities.

Our Favorite Recipes

South Texas Chapter Pioneers collected recipes from telephone pioneers from the southern half of Texas, including Houston, San Antonio, Corpus Christi, Beaumont, Brownsville, and Laredo. This cookbook, published in 2002, is the result of the combined effort of over 18,300 employees and retirees from Southwestern Bell Corporation and its family of companies.

Recipes to Remember

In 2006, SBC Telecom Pioneers Coastal Bend Club #82 compiled recipes from pioneers and friends to honor the memory of one of the guiding lights in the development of the book, Sylvia A. Vasquez. Proceeds of this book were donated to the American Cancer Society in her name.

Beverages and Appetizers

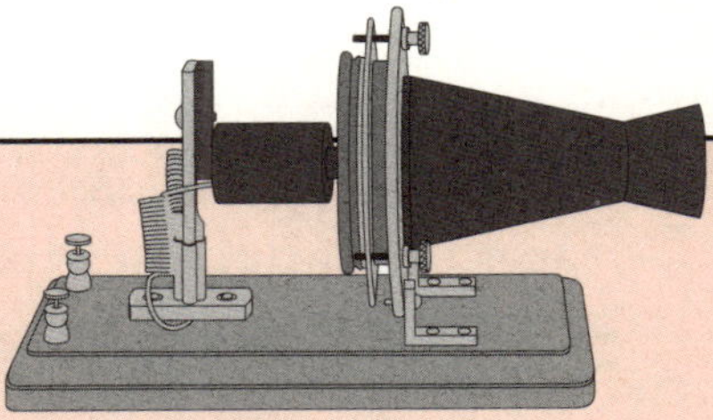

1876
Bell's Centennial Model

"My word! It talks!" exclaimed Emperor Dom Pedro of Brazil when this early phone was demonstrated by Alexander Graham Bell at the Centennial Exposition in Philadelphia on June 25, 1876. One of the judges called the invention "the most wonderful thing in America." Bell's success with the telephone came as a direct result of his attempts to improve the telegraph.

Just three months prior, while working with fellow inventor Thomas Watson, Bell shouted, "Mr. Watson, come here. I want you!" after spilling battery acid on a transmitter. Watson, working in the next room, heard Bell's voice through the wire. Watson had received the first telephone call, and quickly went to answer it.

Sangria

Sangria crossed the Atlantic with the Spanish to Mexico. Fruity and refreshing, it is widely served, the perfect beginning for a Mexican "fiesta."

6 oranges, sliced
3 lemons, sliced
1 lime, sliced
1 cup sugar, or more to taste
½ pint brandy
1 gallon dry red wine

Arrange fruit slices in bottom of very large pitcher or crock. Sprinkle sugar over fruit. Add brandy and allow to sit at least 1 hour. Add wine; stir well and allow to sit 30 minutes. Serve in stemmed glasses over ice. Makes 18 cups.

Donna Wilcox (Cookins for Gulf Coast Council / Red)

Piano Punch

Very pretty in punch bowl or tall pitcher.

4 (6-ounce) cans pink lemonade, undiluted
4 quarts strawberry soda
4 quarts ginger ale
1 (10-ounce) package frozen sweetened strawberries
1 lemon, sliced
6 cups crushed ice

Mix lemonade, soda, ginger ale, and strawberries. Garnish with lemon slices and ice. Makes about 9 quarts.

(Cookins for Gulf Coast Council / Red)

Orange-Banana Flip

2 large oranges, peeled, sectioned, seeded
1 large banana, peeled, sliced
1 cup cold milk
¼ cup sugar (optional)
⅛ teaspoon salt
5–6 ice cubes

Combine all ingredients in electric blender; process until smooth. Makes 1 quart.

Linda Biery (Cookins for Gulf Coast Council / Red)

Garlic Cheese Ball

½ pound Swiss cheese, grated, room temperature
1 (8-ounce) package cream cheese, softened
1 (1-pound) box Velveeta cheese
1 small clove garlic, crushed
Chopped nuts
Paprika

Cream all cheeses together; add garlic and nuts; mix well. Roll into ball or log on wax paper. Sprinkle with paprika; chill.

(Cookins for Gulf Coast Council / Red)

Cheese Ball

3 (8-ounce) packages cream cheese, softened
2 (4-ounce) cans mushrooms, chopped
1 (8-ounce) can chopped black olives
2 (2-ounce) jars dried beef, chopped
6 large fresh green onions with tops, chopped
4 teaspoons Ac'cent
½ cup chopped pecans

Combine all ingredients except pecans. Form into ball; roll in pecans and refrigerate.

(Country Favorites)

Pineapple Cheese Ball

1 (8-ounce) can pineapple chunks, drained completely
2 (8-ounce) packages cream cheese, softened
1 teaspoon seasoned salt
1 tablespoon Worcestershire
¼ cup chopped pecans
2 tablespoons chopped green bell pepper
2½ tablespoons chopped onion

Mix all ingredients with hands. Shape or mold as you desire. Serve with crackers or chips.

(Country Favorites)

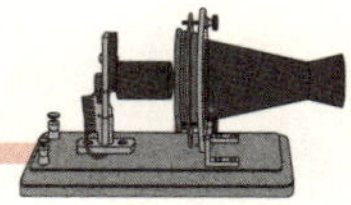

Sweet and Sour Meatballs

MEATBALLS:

1½ pounds ground beef
⅔ cup cracker crumbs
½ cup minced onion
1 egg
1½ teaspoons salt
¼ teaspoon ginger
¼ cup milk

Mix ingredients; shape into balls. Brown in shortening. May be made ahead and refrigerated or frozen.

SAUCE:

1 tablespoon cornstarch
½ cup brown sugar
1 (15-ounce) can pineapple chunks, drained, reserve syrup
⅓ cup apple cider vinegar
1 tablespoon soy sauce
⅓ cup chopped green bell pepper

In saucepan, mix cornstarch and sugar. Stir in syrup, vinegar, and soy sauce. Cook over medium heat, stirring till thick; allow to boil 1 minute. Add meatballs, pineapple chunks, and green pepper; heat thoroughly. Serve in chafing dish.

Earline Greer (Cookins for Gulf Coast Council / Red)

Has any means of communication revolutionized the daily lives of ordinary people more than the telephone? Simply described, it is a system that converts sound, specifically the human voice, to electrical impulses of various frequencies and then back to a tone that sounds like the original voice.

Sausage Balls

Different from most!

1 pound ground pork sausage
½ pound ground beef
¼ teaspoon salt
¼ teaspoon pepper
2 tablespoons shortening
3 cups mashed potatoes
3 eggs
½ cup milk
3 cups bread crumbs

Combine sausage, beef, salt, and pepper; make into 1-inch balls. Brown in shortening; drain; cool. When cool enough to handle, coat with mashed potatoes. Beat eggs and milk together; dip sausage balls in egg mixture and roll in bread crumbs. Let sit 30 minutes. Deep-fry until golden brown. Makes 18–24 balls.

(Country Favorites)

Crunch Swiss/Ham Appetizers

2 cups very stiff mashed potatoes
2 cups finely chopped cooked ham
1 cup shredded Swiss cheese
⅓ cup mayonnaise
1 egg, beaten
½ teaspoon salt
¼ cup minced onion
1 teaspoon prepared mustard
¼ teaspoon pepper
3½ cups crushed cornflakes

Combine all ingredients except cornflakes; chill. Shape into 1-inch balls and roll in cornflakes. Place on greased cookie sheet and bake at 350° for 25–30 minutes. Serve hot. Makes 8 dozen.

(Country Favorites)

Chili-Cheese Squares

5 eggs
¼ cup all-purpose flour
¼ cup butter, melted
½ teaspoon baking powder
Dash of onion or garlic salt
1 (4-ounce) can chopped green chiles
1 (8-ounce) package Monterey Jack cheese, cut into ½-inch cubes
1 (8-ounce) carton small-curd cottage cheese

Beat eggs until light. Whisk in flour, butter, baking powder, and onion or garlic salt until smooth. Stir in chiles, cheese, and cottage cheese. Pour into greased shallow 1½-quart baking dish, square or round. Bake at 350° for 35 minutes, or until firm and well browned. Cut into squares or wedges. Serves 12–15.

(Country Favorites)

Seeded Cheese Rounds

1 cup butter or margarine, softened
4 cups shredded sharp Cheddar cheese, room temperature
2 cups all-purpose flour
⅛ teaspoon cayenne (optional)
Sesame seeds and poppy seeds
Paprika

Cream butter with mixer or food processor using steel blade. Blend in cheese, flour, and cayenne, if used. Chill about 1 hour; shape into 1-inch balls. Sprinkle half of the balls with sesame seeds and remaining half in poppy seeds. Place on ungreased baking sheet 1½ inches apart. Chill 1 hour.

Bake at 400° for 10 minutes; do not brown! The rounds will not be dry when done; cool on baking sheets. Store in airtight containers in cool place. Reheat slightly to serve, if desired. Makes 5 dozen rounds.

(Country Favorites)

Dried Beef Cocktail Spread

- **1 (8-ounce) package cream, cheese softened**
- **2 tablespoons milk**
- **1 (2½-ounce) jar sliced dried beef, chopped**
- **2 tablespoons instant minced onion**
- **2 tablespoons chopped green bell pepper**
- **½ cup sour cream**
- **½ cup chopped pecans**

Blend cream cheese and milk; stir in dried beef, onion, and green pepper; mix well. Stir in sour cream. Spoon into 8-inch pie plate. Sprinkle nuts on top; bake at 350° for 15 minutes; keep warm. Serve with Wheat Thins or Triscuits.

(Cookins for Gulf Coast Council / Blue)

Mexican Roll-Ups

- **1 cup sour cream**
- **1 (8-ounce) package cream cheese, softened**
- **1 (4-ounce) can chopped green chiles, drained**
- **1 (4-ounce) can chopped ripe olives**
- **¼ cup chopped green olives**
- **1 cup grated Cheddar cheese**
- **¼ cup minced onion**
- **1 teaspoon garlic salt**
- **12 burrito-size flour tortillas**

Blend sour cream and cream cheese until smooth. Add remaining ingredients; mix well. Spread cheese mixture on tortillas; roll up and place seam side down in a glass casserole dish. Chill several hours until firm. Remove from dish and slice into ½-inch pieces. Serve with picante sauce.

Note: An electric knife really makes slicing quick and easy.

Winnie Hutsell (Our Favorite Recipes)

Burrito Bites

1 (10-ounce) can Ro-Tel tomatoes
1 cup instant rice
⅓ cup water
1 green bell pepper, diced
2 green onions, sliced
2 cups shredded Cheddar cheese, divided
1 (16-ounce) can ranch-style refried beans
10 (6- to 7-inch) flour tortillas
1 cup salsa

Preheat oven to 350°. Spray a 9x13-inch baking dish with Pam; set aside. In medium saucepan, combine Ro-Tel, rice, and water; heat to a boil. Reduce heat; cover and simmer 1 minute. Remove from heat and let sit 5 minutes, or until all liquid is absorbed. Stir in pepper, onions, and 1 cup cheese. Spread about 3 tablespoons beans over each tortilla to within ⅛ inch from edge. Layer rice mixture over beans; roll up. Place seam side down in prepared baking dish; cover with foil. Bake in preheated oven 25 minutes, or until hot. Cut tortillas into 4 pieces and place on platter. Top with salsa and remaining cheese. Makes 40 bite-size burritos.

Variation: To serve as a delicious entrée, prepare as directed but do not cut. Top with salsa and cheese, return to oven, and bake 5 minutes or till cheese melts.

Ofe Gonzales (Recipes to Remember)

Armadillo Eggs

1 (15-ounce) can jalapeño peppers, stemmed, seeded
½ cup grated Monterey Jack cheese
2 cups grated Cheddar cheese, room temperature
1½ cups Bisquick
½ pound sausage, room temperature
1 package pork Shake 'N Bake

Stuff peppers with Monterey Jack cheese; set aside. Make dough with Cheddar cheese, Bisquick, and sausage (mix with hands). Pinch enough dough to wrap each stuffed pepper (if peppers are large, cut in half). Roll in Shake 'N Bake and place on cookie sheet. Refrigerate a few hours or overnight. Bake at 425° for 20 minutes. Makes about 24.

(Country Favorites)

Jalapeño Peppers–Stuffed

1 (8-ounce) package cream cheese, softened
1 small can ripe olives
1 rib celery, chopped
¼ cup chopped pecans
2 green onion tops, chopped
Salt, pepper, and garlic to taste
½ small jar pimentos
Mayonnaise (enough to stir)
1 can whole jalapeño peppers

Mix all ingredients except peppers. Remove seeds from peppers and stuff with filling.

(Country Favorites)

Nachos Supreme

6 (7-inch) flour tortillas
8 ounces lean ground beef
½ cup salsa
2 cups shredded Mexican-style cheese, divided
2 cups shredded lettuce
1 tomato, chopped
3 green onions, thinly sliced
½ cup sliced pitted ripe olives
Sour cream (optional)
Guacamole (optional)

Preheat oven to 400°. Using pizza cutter, cut each tortilla into 6 wedges. Starting at outside edge of 15-inch round baking stone, arrange wedges in circle with sides overlapping and points toward center. Repeat with remaining wedges to form additional overlapping rows of chips. Bake 8–10 minutes, or until chips are lightly browned and crisp; remove from oven.

Cook ground beef over medium heat until beef is no longer pink; drain. Stir in salsa. Sprinkle 1 cup cheese evenly over hot tortilla chips on baking stone. Top evenly with beef mixture, lettuce, tomato, onions, olives, and remaining 1 cup cheese. Serve with sour cream, guacamole, and additional salsa, if desired.

(Recipes to Remember)

Empanadas Excelentes

½ pound ground beef
¼ cup chopped onion
1½ cups shredded sharp Cheddar cheese
¼ cup ketchup
1 teaspoon chili powder
¼ teaspoon salt
¼ teaspoon Tabasco
Pastry for double crust

Brown meat; drain. Add onion; cook until tender. Stir in cheese, ketchup, and seasonings. Roll pastry to ¼-inch thickness on lightly floured surface. Cut pastry with 3½-inch round cutter. Spoon about 1 teaspoon meat mixture onto center of each round. Fold in half; press edges together with fork. Bake at 450° for 10–12 minutes, or until lightly browned. Serve warm. Makes 3½ dozen.

Martha Sanford (Cookins for Gulf Coast Council / Red)

Mexican Shrimp Cocktail

¼ cup ketchup
¼ cup lime juice
1–2 teaspoons Tabasco
1 pound fresh or frozen shrimp, peeled, deveined, cooked
½ cup chopped tomato
¼ cup chopped onion
¼ cup snipped fresh cilantro
2 avocados, deseeded, peeled, chopped
Lime wedges (optional)
Purple flowering kale (optional)

In large bowl, stir together ketchup, lime juice, and Tabasco. Add shrimp, tomato, onion, and cilantro; toss to coat. Cover and chill 2–4 hours. Just before serving, add avocados; toss to coat. Garnish with lime wedges and flowering kale, if desired. Serve with tortilla chips. Makes 8 appetizer servings.

Cathi Garza (Recipes to Remember)

Tex-Mex Dip

3 medium-size ripe avocados
2 tablespoons lemon juice
½ teaspoon salt
¼ teaspoon pepper
1 cup sour cream
¼ cup mayonnaise or salad dressing
1 package taco seasoning mix
2 (10½-ounce) cans plain or jalapeño-flavored bean dip, or refried beans with jalapeño
1 large bunch green onions with tops, chopped
3 medium tomatoes, cored, halved, coarsely chopped
2 (4-ounce) cans pitted ripe olives, drained, coarsely chopped
1 (8-ounce) package shredded sharp Cheddar cheese
Large round tortilla chips

Peel, pit, and mash avocados in medium-size bowl with lemon juice, salt, and pepper. Combine sour cream, mayonnaise, and taco seasoning; mix well.

Spread bean dip on a large shallow serving platter. Top with seasoned avocado mixture, then sour cream mixture. Sprinkle with chopped onions, tomatoes, and olives; cover with shredded cheese. Serve chilled or at room temperature with round tortilla chips.

Dorothy Reed (Cookins for Gulf Coast Council / Blue)

Baked Cheesy Chili Dip

1 (1-pound) box Velveeta cheese, cubed
1 (10½- or 15-ounce) can chili without beans
1 (4-ounce) can chopped green chiles
½ cup finely chopped onion

Heat oven to 350°. Mix all ingredients; spoon into a 1-quart casserole. Bake 20–25 minutes, or until thoroughly heated. Stir before serving. Serve with firm chips. Makes 4 cups.

(Country Favorites)

Philly Guacamole Dip

2 medium avocados, peeled
1 tablespoon lemon juice
1 (8-ounce) package cream cheese, softened
¼ cup finely chopped onion
½ teaspoon salt
½ teaspoon garlic salt
¼ teaspoon pepper sauce
1 cup chopped tomatoes

Mash avocados with juice. Combine with cream cheese, onion, and seasonings, mixing until well blended. Stir in tomatoes. Serve with chips. Serves 10.

(Country Favorites)

Mollie's Super Dip

1 (8-ounce) package cream cheese, softened
1 (8-ounce) carton sour cream
1 (16-ounce) can refried beans
½ package dry enchilada mix
Hot sauce to taste
1 cup grated Cheddar cheese
1 cup grated Monterey Jack cheese

Combine all ingredients except grated cheeses. Spread in 2 (8-inch) pie pans. Cover with reserved cheeses. Bake 15–20 minutes at 350°. Serve with chips. Serves 8–12.

Star Meyer Kord (Our Favorite Recipes)

1015 Sweet Onion Dip

½ cup sugar
1 cup apple cider vinegar
2 cups water
1 large 1015 or Vidalia onion, finely chopped
½ cup mayonnaise
½ teaspoon dill weed
Ritz Crackers for dipping

In medium bowl, mix together sugar, apple cider vinegar, and water; set aside. Stir onions into mixture and marinate overnight. Before serving, drain well. Stir in mayonnaise and dill. Serve with crackers.

Sugar Roberts (Our Favorite Recipes)

Hot Broccoli Dip

1 (20-ounce) package frozen broccoli cuts (not chopped)
2 sticks butter
1 large onion, chopped
4 or 5 large celery ribs, chopped
1 (8-ounce) can sliced mushrooms, drained
2 (10¾-ounce) cans cream of mushroom soup
1 pound American cheese

Cook broccoli according to package directions, but only cook ½ required time. Drain in colander and drain further on paper towels; set aside. Melt butter in heavy oven-proof saucepan. Sauté chopped onion and celery until golden brown. Pat mushrooms with paper towels and add to skillet; cook 3–4 minutes; add soup. Cut cheese into 1-inch squares; add to soup mixture. Add broccoli and mix lightly. Cover skillet and place in 300° oven until cheese melts, about 25 minutes; do not overcook. Place in chafing dish and serve with corn chips.

Note: May thin with cream, beer, or more soup. If too thin, add more cheese.

Mrs. Henry M. Brau (Cookins for Gulf Coast Council / Blue)

The telephone truly changed the face of America from the day it was introduced. From a single unit in 1876, the count grew to eleven million telephones nationwide by 1915! In honor of his invention's tremendous impact, every telephone in America stopped ringing for one minute during Alexander Graham Bell's funeral in 1922.

Cucumber Dip

1 (8-ounce) package cream cheese, softened
2 small cucumbers, finely grated
½ teaspoon Worcestershire
Dash of celery salt
Dash of garlic salt
¼ cup onion flakes
1 tablespoon mayonnaise
Several drops hot sauce
1 green onion, finely chopped

Combine all ingredients in bowl with electric mixer. Chill.

Ricebird Club (Cookins for Gulf Coast Council / Red)

Curry Dip

½ teaspoon garlic salt
1 onion, grated
3 teaspoons curry powder
1 pint mayonnaise
3 teaspoons Worcestershire

Combine all ingredients well; chill. Serve with fresh vegetables of choice.

Tiny Ponder (Cookins for Gulf Coast Council / Red)

Oscar Night Crab Dip

2 cups lump crabmeat, lightly sprinkled with lime juice
2 (8-ounce) tubs whipped cream cheese
1 cup mayonnaise
3 tablespoons milk
1 tablespoon hot sauce
4 green onions, minced
¼ teaspoon celery salt
¼ teaspoon paprika
Pepper to taste
1 cup boiled, deveined shrimp

Pulverize lump crabmeat in deep bowl with electric hand mixer. Add cream cheese and mayonnaise; blend thoroughly. Add milk, hot sauce, green onions, and seasonings. Pulverize shrimp by hand and add to mixture; blend well. Chill and serve with crisp toast or crackers. Also good as spread on celery sticks.

(Cookins for Gulf Coast Council / Red)

Salmon Dip

1 (6½-ounce) can salmon, drained
1 (8-ounce) package cream cheese, softened
3 tablespoons chopped green onions
1 teaspoon lemon juice
2 or 3 drops liquid smoke
1 round of pumpernickel bread

Combine salmon, cream cheese, and remaining ingredients. Mix well. Cut a circle in top of bread and pull out enough to make a well. Serve dip in well. Refrigerate for hours.

Lee Tates (Our Favorite Recipes)

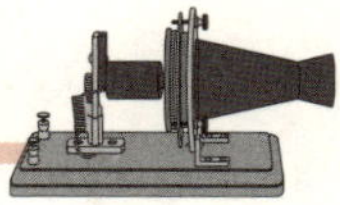

Donna's Bean Dip

1 (10¾-ounce) can condensed black bean soup
1 (10¾-ounce) can condensed bean with bacon soup
¼ cup water
1 teaspoon dry mustard
½ teaspoon cayenne pepper
½ teaspoon chili powder
2 cloves garlic, pressed
4–5 drops Tabasco
1 tablespoon vinegar
½ cup sour cream

In saucepan, heat all ingredients except sour cream, stirring constantly. Add sour cream and simmer 10 minutes. Can be served warm or chilled with tostados. Makes 3 cups.

Donna Wilcox (Cookins for Gulf Coast Council / Red)

Refried Bean Dip

1 stick butter
⅓–½ cup finely chopped onion
1 large can refried beans
2 cups shredded sharp Cheddar cheese
½ teaspoon garlic juice

Melt butter and sauté onions until translucent. Mix in beans until well blended. Cook on low heat, stirring occasionally. Add cheese and garlic juice; stir until all cheese is melted. Serve with corn or tortilla chips.

(Country Favorites)

Pico de Gallo

¼ medium onion
½ medium-size tomato
Cilantro to taste
4 serrano peppers
Juice from ½ lime
Salt to taste

Chop first 4 items well; squeeze lime juice over; sprinkle with salt; mix together. Serve with tortilla chips.

Belinda Estrada (Recipes to Remember)

Fresh Salsa

2 large tomatoes, finely chopped
1 (6-ounce) can chopped black olives
1 (4-ounce) can chopped green chiles
4 green onions, chopped
3 tablespoons olive oil
1½ tablespoons vinegar
1 teaspoon garlic salt

Mix all ingredients together. Serve with tortilla chips.

Barbara Baldwin (Our Favorite Recipes)

Pepperoni Stromboli

2 (1-pound) loaves frozen bread dough, thawed
½ cup spaghetti sauce
½ teaspoon dried oregano
4 ounces sliced pepperoni sausage
2 cups shredded mozzarella cheese
⅓ cup grated Parmesan cheese

Preheat oven to 350°. Punch dough down. On a lightly floured surface, roll each loaf into 8x20-inch rectangle. Place one rectangle on a greased baking sheet. Spread spaghetti sauce in a 4x18-inch strip down the center. Sprinkle with oregano, pepperoni, and mozzarella cheese.

Fold long sides of dough up toward filling; set aside. Cut remaining rectangle into 3 strips. Loosely braid strips; pinch ends to seal. Place bread on top of cheese; pinch braid to dough to seal. Sprinkle with Parmesan cheese. Bake in preheated oven for 30 minutes, or until golden brown. Cut into individual serving slices.

Linda O'Dell (Our Favorite Recipes)

Very early telephones were far different than even what you may think of as "old fashioned" phones. For instance, some early models had only one port for both speaking and hearing. Users had to speak into the receiver, then move it to their ear to wait for a response.

Finger Pizzas

½ cup chopped green bell pepper
½ cup chopped onion
1–2 tablespoons oil
½ pound sausage
½ pound ground beef
1 (10-ounce) can Ro-Tel tomatoes
½ cup chopped mushrooms
1 (8-ounce) can tomato sauce
1 pound American cheese, grated
1 pound sharp Cheddar cheese, grated
1 cup chopped olives
5 (20-count) packages small party rolls

Sauté pepper and onion in oil; set aside. In same pan, brown sausage and ground meat; drain. Combine all ingredients except rolls. Scoop out center of rolls with spoon, making well in tops. Preheat oven to 350°. Fill rolls with pizza mix and bake 10 minutes. Pepperoni slices may be put on top, if desired. Mixture may be made ahead and frozen or refrigerated several days. Serve piping hot. Makes 100.

(Recipes to Remember)

Fruit Pizza

1 (20-ounce) roll refrigerated sugar cookie dough
1 (8-ounce) package cream cheese, softened
⅓ cup sugar
½ teaspoon vanilla
1 banana, sliced
Lemon juice
2 kiwi fruits, sliced
1 cup sliced fresh strawberries
½ cup fresh blueberries
½ cup orange marmalade or peach preserves
1–2 tablespoons water

Press cookie dough evenly onto a lightly greased 12-inch pizza pan; prick with fork. Bake at 375° for 10–12 minutes; cool.

In a bowl, combine cream cheese, sugar, and vanilla until smooth. Spread over cooled crust. Toss banana slices with lemon juice to prevent discoloration.

Arrange kiwi fruit, strawberries, bananas, and blueberries on top of cream cheese mixture. In a small bowl, combine orange marmalade and water; spoon over fruit. Chill 1 hour, or until serving time. Serves 8–10.

Winnie Hutsell (Our Favorite Recipes)

Dill-Pickle Okra

3 pounds young okra
1 quart water
2 cups white vinegar
½ cup salt
Dill or dill seeds (per jar)
Garlic cloves (per jar)
Celery leaves (per jar) (optional)

Wash and trim okra; pack into sterilized quart or pint jars. Combine water, vinegar, and salt in saucepan; bring to a boil. Add 1 teaspoon dill or dill seeds, 1 or 2 cloves garlic, and some celery leaves to each jar. Pour hot liquid over okra, leaving ¼-inch headspace. Place lids and bands on jars, screwing bands on tight. Store at least 3 weeks before serving.

Catherine Losack (Cookins for Gulf Coast Council / Red)

Spicy Glazed Nuts

¼ cup corn syrup
2 tablespoons margarine or butter
2 tablespoons orange juice
1 teaspoon coriander
¼ teaspoon ground red pepper (cayenne)
½ teaspoon salt
2 cups hazelnuts or walnut halves

Heat oven to 350°. Grease 10x15-inch baking pan. In medium saucepan, combine corn syrup, margarine, and orange juice. Cook over medium heat until margarine is melted, stirring constantly. Stir in coriander, ground red pepper, and salt; blend well. Add nuts; stir to coat evenly. Spread nuts on greased pan. Bake at 350° for 15–20 minutes, or until golden brown and glazed, stirring occasionally. Store in tightly covered container. Makes 2 cups.

(Recipes to Remember)

Bread and Breakfast

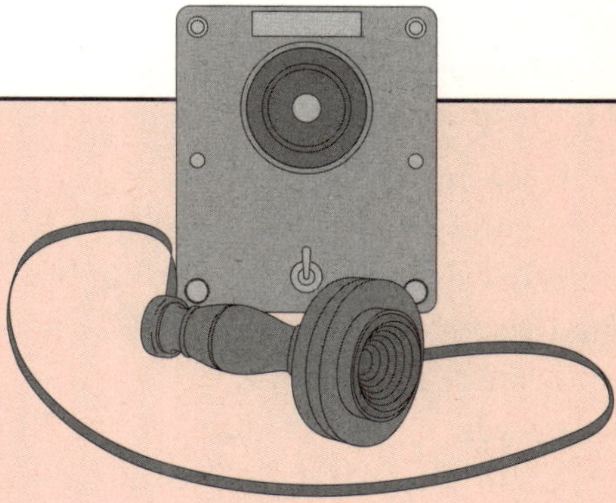

1878
Butterstamp

The first telephone with a combined receiver-transmitter that could be held in the hand looked like a butterstamp—hence its name. You talked into one end, turned the instrument around, and listened to the other end. The push button signaled the operator. This model was in service when the world's first commercial switchboard opened in New Haven, Connecticut, in 1878. Western Union opened the first large city exchange in San Francisco that same year. The public switched telephone network was born; no longer limited to people on the same wire, folks could now talk to many others on different lines.

Cheese Caraway Batter Bread

1 package active dry yeast
1¼ cups warm water
1 cup shredded sharp Cheddar cheese
2 tablespoons shortening
2 tablespoons sugar
2 teaspoons salt
1 teaspoon caraway seeds
2⅔ cups all-purpose flour, divided
Melted butter

In large mixer bowl, dissolve yeast in warm water; add cheese, shortening, sugar, salt, caraway seeds, and 2 cups flour. Blend ½ minute on low speed, scraping bowl constantly. Beat 2 minutes on medium speed, scraping bowl occasionally. Stir in remaining flour until smooth. Scrape batter from side of bowl; cover; let rise in warm place until double, about 30 minutes.

Stir down batter by beating about 25 strokes. Spread evenly in greased 5x9-inch loaf pan; smooth out top of batter by patting into shape with floured hands. Cover; let rise until double, about 40 minutes.

Heat oven to 375°. Bake 45 minutes, or until loaf sounds hollow when tapped. Brush top with melted butter. Remove loaf from pan; cool on wire rack.

Cutting tip: Turn bread upside down to cut; use a serrated knife with sawing motion.

Susan Rea (Cookins for Gulf Coast Council / Blue)

Butterhorn Rolls

1 package dry yeast
½ cup tap water
½ cup milk, scalded
½ cup butter
⅓ cup sugar
¾ teaspoon salt
1 egg
4 cups all-purpose flour, divided

Dissolve yeast in water. Pour hot milk over butter, sugar, and salt. Cool to lukewarm. Add yeast, egg, and 2 cups flour; beat well. Add enough remaining flour that it will not stick to bowl. Pour dough out and knead lightly. Place dough in greased bowl; cover and let rise until doubled in size, about an hour. Divide dough in half. Roll each piece in pie shape, about 12 inches across. Cut each in 12 pie-shaped pieces.

With hands, roll each pie-shaped piece from the wide end and place pointed end down on a greased baking sheet. Let rise until doubled in size, about 30 minutes.

Bake in hot 400° oven about 15 minutes, until lightly brown. If you make regular rolls with this dough, be sure to roll the dough with the rolling pin before shaping into rolls, otherwise rolls won't be very good; I know this from experience.

Billy Cash (Our Favorite Recipes)

Good Biscuits

4 cups Pioneer Biscuit Mix
¾ cup sour cream
1 cup club soda

After mixing ingredients, knead on a floured board (using some of the dry biscuit mix) and pinch off amount and place in lightly greased pan. Cast-iron skillets give biscuits a good "crusty" bottom. Bake as directed on box. If you like, brush 'em with butter for Popeye's-type biscuits. Makes about 2 dozen.

(Country Favorites)

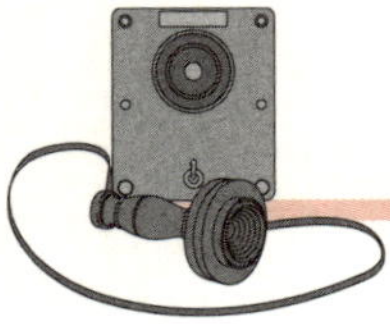

Fiesta Chili Cornbread

2 (8-ounce) packages corn muffin mix
2 eggs, lightly beaten
⅔ cup milk
1 (11-ounce) can Mexican-style corn, drained
1 (15-ounce) can chili without beans
1 cup shredded Cheddar cheese
1 cup shredded Monterey Jack cheese
½ cup sliced green onions with tops
½ cup chopped pitted ripe olives, drained
Sour cream (optional)

Preheat oven to 350°. Lightly spray 2 flan pans with vegetable oil. Combine corn muffin mix, eggs, milk, and corn; mix until well blended. Divide batter evenly between flan pans; bake 20 minutes. Remove to cooling rack; cool 10 minutes; turn out into serving plates.

Heat chili over medium heat until hot. Divide between cornbread crusts. Top with cheeses, green onions, and olives. Garnish with sour cream, if desired. Serves 8–10.

(Recipes to Remember)

Mexican Cornbread

1½ cups cornmeal
½ cup all-purpose flour
3 teaspoons baking powder
1 teaspoon salt
1 cup buttermilk
1 egg
1 cup whole-kernel corn
3 jalapeño peppers, seeded, chopped
1 sweet bell pepper, chopped
½ cup oil
½ cup chopped onion
½ cup chopped pimentos

Combine all ingredients. Bake in hot greased skillet or pan in 425° oven 20–25 minutes. Serves 6–8.

(Country Favorites)

Mexican Cornbread

2 (7-ounce) packages Mexican-style cornbread mix
3 eggs
1½ cups milk
1 pound sausage, cooked
1 (15-ounce) can cream-style corn
1 pound grated sharp Cheddar cheese
Chopped onion and green bell pepper, to taste

Mix all ingredients together; bake in 9x13-inch pan at 350° for 1 hour.

Nelda Aguilera (Recipes to Remember)

Broccoli Cornbread

½ cup butter, melted
⅓ cup chopped onion
1 teaspoon salt
¾ cup cottage cheese
1 (10-ounce) package frozen chopped broccoli, thawed, drained
4 eggs, slightly beaten
1 (8-ounce) package corn muffin mix

In mixing bowl, combine melted butter, onion, salt, cheese, broccoli, and eggs; blend. Stir in muffin mix. Pour into greased 9x13-inch baking pan. Bake at 400° for 20–25 minutes. Cut into squares. Serves 12.

(Country Favorites)

Texas Hush Puppies

2 cups cornmeal
½ cup all-purpose flour
1 teaspoon baking soda
1 tablespoon baking powder
1 tablespoon salt
1 egg, beaten
6 tablespoons finely chopped onion
2 cups buttermilk

Combine all ingredients; drop by spoon into hot oil and cook until brown.

Helen Thiel (Cookins for Gulf Coast Council / Blue)

Flour Tortillas

1½ cups boiling water
3 cups all-purpose flour
1 tablespoon baking powder
1 teaspoon salt
½ cup shortening

Use wire whisk to mix hot water and flour; add remaining ingredients; let rest 10–15 minutes. Form dough by kneading with hands until smooth and soft. Let rest another 5–10 minutes. Shape dough into small balls. Using a rolling pin, roll balls to about 5 inches in diameter. Cook on hot griddle, 1½–2 minutes on each side.

Esteban Mendoza (Recipes to Remember)

Zucchini Bread

3 eggs, beaten
1 cup oil
2 cups granulated sugar
2 teaspoons vanilla
2 cups shredded zucchini
1 cup crushed pineapple
3 cups all-purpose flour, sifted
2 teaspoons baking soda
1 teaspoon salt
½ teaspoon baking powder
1½ teaspoons cinnamon
¾ teaspoon nutmeg
1 cup coarsely chopped walnuts

Mix eggs, oil, sugar, and vanilla; beat until thick and foamy. Stir in zucchini and pineapple. Combine remaining ingredients and stir gently into zucchini mixture just until blended. Bake in 2 well-greased 5x9-inch loaf pans. Bake at 350° for 1 hour, or until done. Cool in pans 10 minutes; turn out on wire rack to cool.

Winnie Hutsell (Our Favorite Recipes)

Cranberry Bread

2 cups all-purpose flour
1½ teaspoons baking powder
½ teaspoon salt
½ teaspoon baking soda
1 cup sugar
1 orange, juiced, rind grated, with enough boiling water added to make ¾ cup
2 tablespoons shortening
1 egg, beaten
1 cup whole fresh cranberries
1 cup chopped nuts

Sift together dry ingredients into bowl. Add orange juice, grated rind and water, and shortening; stir. Add beaten egg, cranberries, and nuts. Pour into greased 5x9-inch loaf pan and bake at 325° for 45 minutes to 1 hour. Serves 10–12.

(Country Favorites)

Orange Bundt Biscuits

¾ cup sugar
1 tablespoon orange zest
½ cup chopped pecans
1 (3-ounce) package cream cheese, cut into 20 chunks
2 (10-count) cans buttermilk biscuits
½ cup butter, melted
1 cup sifted powdered sugar
2 tablespoons orange juice

Lightly grease a Bundt pan. Preheat oven to 350°. Mix together sugar, orange zest, and pecans. Push a chunk of cheese into side of each biscuit and squeeze shut; leave in biscuit shape. Dip each biscuit in melted butter; roll in sugar mixture. Stand up each biscuit in wheel fashion around bottom of Bundt pan, making only one row. Bake at 350° for 30–45 minutes; let cool 5 minutes. Invert onto platter. Mix powdered sugar and orange juice together. Spread over inverted biscuits.

(Country Favorites)

Apple Raisin Bran Muffins

1½ cups shredded wheat bran cereal
1 cup skim milk
¼ cup Promise spread, melted
½ cup honey
1 large cooking apple, peeled, cored, grated
¾ cup raisins
1 large egg, well beaten
1 teaspoon cinnamon
1¼ cups all-purpose flour
2 teaspoons baking powder
½ teaspoon baking soda

Heat oven to 400°. Lightly grease 12 muffin cups. In large bowl, soak cereal in milk 5 minutes. Stir in Promise, honey, apple, raisins, egg, and cinnamon. In another bowl, combine remaining ingredients. Fold flour mixture into apple bran mixture, just enough to moisten; do not overmix. Evenly distribute among muffin cups. Bake 20 minutes, or until done.

(Country Favorites)

Bohemian Coffee Cake

2½ cups all-purpose flour, sifted
1 teaspoon salt
1 teaspoon cinnamon
1 teaspoon nutmeg
1 cup brown sugar
1 cup granulated sugar
2 eggs
1 cup oil
1 cup buttermilk
1 teaspoon baking soda
1 teaspoon vanilla
1 cup flaked coconut
1 cup chopped pecans

Sift flour and mix in salt and spices; set aside. Cream sugars, eggs, and oil. Beat buttermilk and soda well by hand; add creamed mixture; gradually add dry ingredients. Add vanilla, coconut, and pecans. Mix and bake in 2 (9-inch) greased and floured layer pans or tube pan at 350° for 50 minutes.

FROSTING:

1 (8-ounce) package cream cheese, softened
1 stick margarine, softened
1 (1-pound) box powdered sugar
2 teaspoons vanilla

Mix ingredients well; frost cake. Top with additional chopped pecans, coconut, or cherries, if desired.

Joyce Abraham (Cookins for Gulf Coast Council / Red)

Cranberry Coffee Cake

1 cup butter, softened
1 cup sugar
2 eggs
2 cups self-rising flour
1 (8-ounce) carton sour cream
1 teaspoon almond extract
1 (15-ounce) can whole cranberry sauce
1 cup chopped pecans

Preheat oven to 325°. Cream butter, sugar, and eggs together. Add flour and sour cream alternately. Add almond extract. Butter and flour 9x13-inch baking pan. Spread mixture in bottom of pan; only go halfway up the pan. Dollop cranberry sauce on top of batter. Sprinkle chopped pecans over cranberry sauce. Bake 40 minutes, or until cake is golden brown and toothpick inserted comes out clean.

FROSTING:

1 cup powdered sugar
1 teaspoon almond extract
Half-and-half to make desired consistency

Mix together and drizzle over cake. Serves 15.

Barbara Wilson (Our Favorite Recipes)

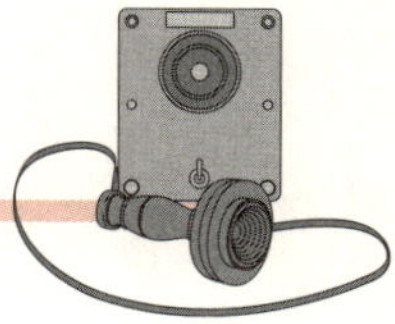

Fluffy Flapjacks

1¼ cups all-purpose flour
2 teaspoons baking soda
2 tablespoons sugar
½ teaspoon salt
1 cup buttermilk
2 tablespoons butter, melted
1 egg

Mix dry ingredients; combine buttermilk, melted butter, and egg; add to dry ingredients. Batter will be thick. Bake on ungreased griddle. Makes 8–10.

(Cookins for Gulf Coast Council / Red)

Apple and Raisin Oven Pancake

1 large baking apple, cored, thinly sliced
⅓ cup golden raisins
2 tablespoons packed brown sugar
½ teaspoon ground cinnamon
4 eggs
⅔ cup milk
⅔ cup all-purpose flour
2 tablespoons butter, melted
Powdered sugar (optional)

Preheat oven to 350°. Spray 9-inch pie plate with nonstick cooking spray. Combine apple, raisins, brown sugar, and cinnamon in medium bowl. Transfer to prepared pie plate. Bake uncovered, 10–15 minutes, or until apples begin to soften. Remove from oven; increase oven temperature to 450°.

Whisk eggs, milk, flour, and butter in medium bowl until blended. Pour batter over apple mixture. Bake 15 minutes, or until pancake is golden brown. Sprinkle with powdered sugar, if desired.

GeraLyn "Gerri" Gray (Our Favorite Recipes)

Crusty Cheese Rings

2 cups all-purpose flour
1 cup butter
½ cup whipping cream
2 teaspoons white vinegar
½ cup grated Swiss, Monterey Jack, or Parmesan cheese
1 egg white, slightly beaten
Additional cheese for topping

Combine flour and butter, cutting butter in until slightly smaller than peas. Mix in cream and vinegar with a fork. Stir in cheese, distributing evenly. Form dough into a ball. Roll dough out on lightly floured surface to ¼-inch thickness. Cut into rings using doughnut cutter. Repeat with leftover dough. Place rings and centers (holes) on ungreased baking sheet about 1 inch apart. Chill 30 minutes. Brush tops with egg white; sprinkle with additional cheese. Bake at 450° for 10 minutes, or until lightly browned. Serve hot. Makes 30 rings.

(Country Favorites)

Breakfast Tacos

1 pound hot pork sausage
1 (32-ounce) bag frozen hashbrown potatoes
1 green bell pepper, chopped
1 red bell pepper, chopped
1 onion, chopped
3 celery ribs, finely chopped
6 eggs, beaten
1 pound Cheddar cheese, grated
Flour tortillas
Picante sauce

Brown sausage in frying pan; drain. Add hashbrowns, peppers, onion, celery, and eggs. Butter or spray a 9x13-inch or larger casserole. Place taco mixture in casserole, and bake at 350° for 45 minutes. Top with cheese and heat till melted.

To serve, place a large scoop of potato mixture on warmed tortilla; add picante sauce, if desired, roll up, and enjoy. Serves 6–8.

(Country Favorites)

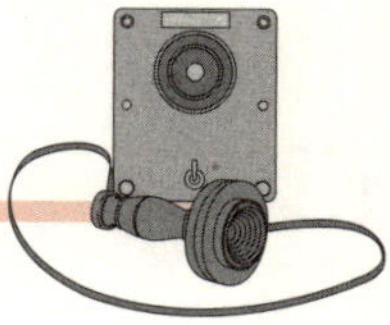

Egg and Sausage Strata

12 slices white bread, crusts removed, cubed
1½ pounds bulk pork sausage
⅓ cup chopped onion
¼ cup chopped green bell pepper
1 (2-ounce) jar chopped pimentos, drained
6 eggs
3 cups milk
2 teaspoons Worcestershire
1 teaspoon dry mustard
½ teaspoon salt
¼ teaspoon pepper
¼ teaspoon dried oregano

Line a greased 9x13-inch pan with bread cubes; set aside. In skillet, brown sausage with onion and green pepper; drain. Stir in pimentos; sprinkle over bread.

In a bowl, beat eggs, milk, Worcestershire, mustard, salt, pepper, and oregano. Pour over sausage mixture; cover and refrigerate overnight.

Bake, covered, at 325° for 1 hour and 20 minutes. Uncover and bake for 10 minutes longer, or until knife inserted near center comes out clean. Let stand 10 minutes before serving. Makes 12–15 servings.

(Country Favorites)

Tony's Rainy Sunday Brunch

Shrimp quiche eaten by real men everywhere!

3 eggs
½ pint whipping cream
Dash of nutmeg
Salt and fresh-ground pepper to taste
1 small onion, finely chopped
½ cup shredded mozzarella cheese
½ cup shredded Swiss cheese
½ cup finely chopped fresh mushrooms
1 cup small shrimp, cooked
1 (9-inch) pie shell, unbaked

Beat eggs, whipping cream, and spices with whisk. Combine remaining ingredients in pastry shell. Pour egg mixture over filling and bake in 350° oven 45–55 minutes, or until set. Serve with fresh melon balls, bagel with cream cheese, and spicy Bloody Marys. Serves 6.

Tony Bernardoni (Cookins for Gulf Coast Council / Red)

Hashbrown Breakfast Casserole

1 (16-ounce) package hashbrowns
¾ cup shredded Cheddar or Monterey Jack cheese
½ pound ham, diced
¼ cup finely chopped onion
4 eggs, lightly beaten
⅛ teaspoon salt
¼ teaspoon pepper
1 (10-ounce) can Ro-Tel tomatoes, drained

Grease 2-quart casserole or 7x11-inch baking pan. Spread hashbrown potatoes in pan. Sprinkle cheese, ham, and onion on top. In small bowl, mix eggs, salt, pepper, and Ro-Tel; pour over mixture in pan. Cover and refrigerate until ready to bake. Preheat oven to 350°; bake for 40–50 minutes, until set in the middle and lightly brown on top. Serves 6–8.

Sylvia Vasquez (Recipes to Remember)

Chile Relleno Bake

½ pound ground beef
½ pound chorizo or pork sausage
1 cup chopped onion
2 cloves garlic, minced
2 (4-ounce) cans whole green chiles, drained, seeded, divided
2 cups shredded Cheddar cheese, divided
4 eggs
¼ cup all-purpose flour
1½ cups milk
½ teaspoon salt
Hot pepper sauce to taste

In large skillet, crumble together beef and sausage. Cook over medium heat, stirring till meat is browned. Add onion and garlic; cook till onion is soft; drain. Line 9x9-inch greased baking dish with half the chiles; top with 1½ cups cheese. Add meat mixture and top with remaining chiles; set aside. Beat together eggs and flour until smooth; add milk, salt, and hot pepper sauce; blend well. Pour egg mixture over casserole. Bake, uncovered, at 350° for 40 minutes, or until knife inserted off center comes out clean. Sprinkle with remaining cheese on top. Let stand 5 minutes before serving. Serves 6.

(Country Favorites)

Wagon Wheel Sausage Pie

1 (12-ounce) package little sizzlers skinless pork sausage
3 cups frozen loose-pack hashbrown potatoes
½ cup chopped green onions with tops
2 tablespoons plus ⅓ cup milk, divided
½ teaspoon salt
¼ teaspoon pepper
1 (8-ounce) package cream cheese, softened
¾ cup Bisquick baking mix
2 eggs, beaten

Cook sausage till very light brown; drain. Generously grease (10-inch) pie plate; spread with potatoes. Mix onions, 2 tablespoons milk, salt, pepper, and cream cheese; spread over potatoes. Arrange sausages over potatoes. Beat baking mix with remaining ⅓ cup milk and eggs with wire whisk or hand beater until almost smooth, about 1 minute; pour around sausages. Bake, uncovered, till edge is light brown and center is set, 25–30 minutes. Serves 6.

(Country Favorites)

Breakfast Casserole

(The Pizza Thing)

1 small roll Jimmy Dean's sausage
7 large eggs
1 (8-ounce) can Grands buttermilk biscuits
1 medium-size jar picante salsa, mild
1 small jar picante salsa, hot
1 (4-ounce) bag shredded Cheddar or Monterey Jack cheese, divided

Brown sausage; crumble and drain; set aside. Scramble eggs, very, very softly (they should be runny). Stir eggs in with sausage; set aside. Tear biscuits into pieces in large bowl. Add mild salsa to biscuits; stir. Add egg-sausage mixture to biscuits, then hot salsa; stir. Add ¼ the cheese; stir. Pour mixture into greased casserole dish and bake at 375° for 45–60 minutes. Sprinkle with remaining cheese and bake about 5 minutes, or long enough to melt and slightly brown the cheese.

Marlene LaGrone (Our Favorite Recipes)

Toasted Cheese Sandwiches

1½ loaves day-old bread
1 pound sharp Cracker Barrel cheese, grated
3 sticks margarine, softened
1 teaspoon onion powder
1½ teaspoons Worcestershire
1¼ teaspoons dill weed
¾ teaspoon Tabasco
Dash of cayenne pepper

Assemble bread in stacks of 3; remove crust. Combine remaining ingredients and spread in between slices and on sides and top of bread stacks. Bake at 325° for 20 minutes.

Note: Can be made ahead and frozen. Place on cookie sheets until well frozen, then place in freezer bags.

(Country Favorites)

Apple Spice Syrup

This syrup has just the right sweetness to compliment your favorite pancakes or waffles. The spicy apple flavor is great for autumn breakfast or whenever you'd like something a bit different.

¼ cup packed brown sugar
2 tablespoons cornstarch
¼ teaspoon ground allspice
⅛ teaspoon ground nutmeg
1¾ cups apple juice or cider

In saucepan, combine brown sugar, cornstarch, allspice, and nutmeg; mix well. Add juice or cider; cook and stir over medium heat until syrup is bubbly and slightly thickened. Makes 1¾ cups.

(Country Favorites)

Pineapple Orange Sauce

1 (20-ounce) can pineapple chunks, undrained
½ cup fresh orange juice
1 teaspoon grated orange peel
1 tablespoon cornstarch
1 tablespoon sugar
1 teaspoon ground ginger

Combine pineapple, orange juice, and peel in saucepan with remaining ingredients. Cook, stirring, until sauce boils and thickens; cool. Serve over ice cream, frozen yogurt, pancakes, or waffles. Makes 8 servings.

(Country Favorites)

Soups, Stews, and Chilies

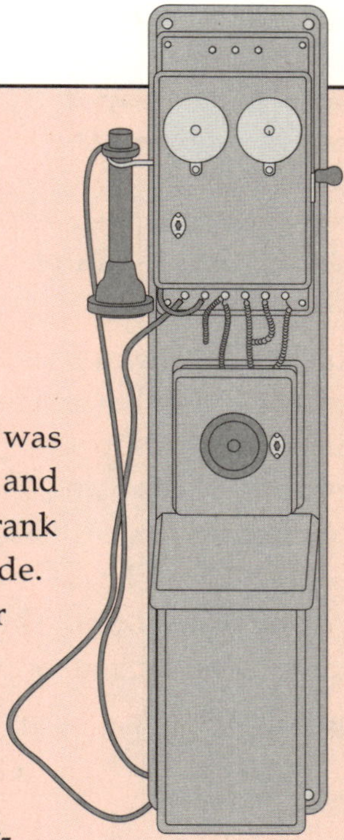

1882
Three-Box

This oak-encased instrument was the standard for many years and one of the first to place the crank more conveniently on the side. The top box contained a ringer and a switchhook. The middle box was a Blake transmitter, which was known for its improved voice clarity. The bottom, a cover for a wet cell battery, doubled as a writing shelf. To place a call, you turned the crank to ring the operator, then picked up the receiver. The operator would then answer and connect you to the party you wished to call. To signal the operator to disconnect the call, you would hang up the receiver and turn the crank to produce a short ring. This was called "ringing off."

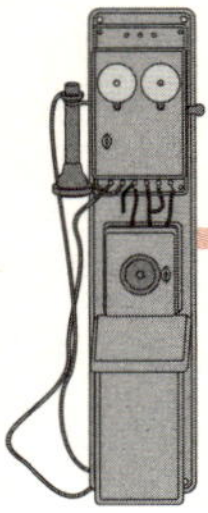

Tortilla Soup

1 whole chicken
2 bay leaves
2 cloves garlic, chopped
2 teaspoons garlic powder
1 tablespoon cumin
1 tablespoon black pepper
2 tablespoons chopped cilantro
1 tablespoon salt
1 cup fresh chopped, peeled tomatoes, or 1 (14½-ounce) can diced tomatoes
1 (10-ounce) can Snappy Tom tomato juice
1 (4-ounce) can chopped green chiles
1 teaspoon chili powder
1 cup chopped white onion
2 teaspoons Worcestershire
6 corn tortillas
Grated Monterey Jack cheese
Lime juice

Cover chicken with water; add bay leaves, garlic, garlic powder, cumin, pepper, cilantro, and salt. Boil till tender; remove from broth and debone; return to pot and add remaining ingredients except tortillas, cheese, and lime juice. Simmer 1 hour. Ten minutes before hour is up, cut about 6 corn tortillas into strips and add to soup. Sprinkle cheese over bowls of soup before serving. Squeeze a few drops of lime juice into each bowl; or if desired, put wedges of lime on table to add per taste. Serves 8.

Note: You may also add fresh avocado or pico de gallo to the soup.

Gale Kercheval (Our Favorite Recipes)

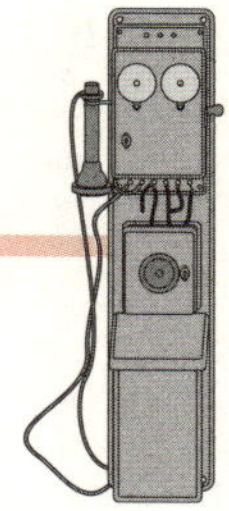

Taco Soup

2 pounds lean ground beef
1 onion, chopped
2 teaspoons seasoning salt
1 (15-ounce) can kidney beans
1 (15-ounce) can pinto beans
2 (16-ounce) cans stewed tomatoes
1 (15-ounce) can corn or hominy, drained
1 (15-ounce) can tomato juice
1 (4-ounce) can diced green chiles
1 package taco seasoning mix
1 package ranch dressing mix

Brown meat and onion in large skillet. Season with seasoning salt. Add remaining ingredients; mix well. Simmer about 45 minutes. Can be served with crackers or over corn chips. Serves a lot.

Martha Manley (Our Favorite Recipes)

Jalapeño-Potato Soup

1 medium onion, chopped
¼ cup butter
5 pounds Russet potatoes, peeled, cubed
8 cups chicken broth
1 teaspoon comino
¼–½ cup coarsely chopped pickled jalapeños, with juice
Pinch of baking soda
4 cups evaporated milk
Salt and pepper to taste

In large stockpot, sauté onion in butter until just tender. Add potatoes, chicken broth, and comino. Cover and cook until potatoes are tender, 20–30 minutes. Add jalapeños, soda, and milk. Coarsely mash potatoes with a potato masher. Stir well; add salt and pepper to taste. Simmer 15 minutes, stirring frequently. Garnish with dollop of sour cream and chopped green onions. Serves 16–18.

(Country Favorites)

Baked Potato Soup

4 large baking potatoes
⅔ cup butter
⅔ cup all-purpose flour
6 cups milk
¾ teaspoon salt
¾ teaspoon pepper
4–8 green onions, divided
16 slices bacon, cooked, crumbled, divided
1½ cups shredded Cheddar cheese, divided
1½ cups sour cream

Wash potatoes and prick several times with fork. Bake at 400° for 1 hour, or until done; let cool. Peel and partially mash; leave chunks. Melt butter in saucepan over low heat. Add flour, stirring until smooth. Cook 1 minute, stirring constantly; gradually add milk. Cook over medium heat, stirring constantly, until mixture thickens and bubbles. Add potatoes, salt, pepper, half the green onions, ½ cup bacon, and 1 cup cheese. Cook until thoroughly heated; stir in sour cream; do not boil. Add extra milk, if needed, for desired thickness. Serve with remaining onions, bacon, and cheese, or you can put all in soup at one time. Serves 8.

Ofe Gonzales (Recipes to Remember)

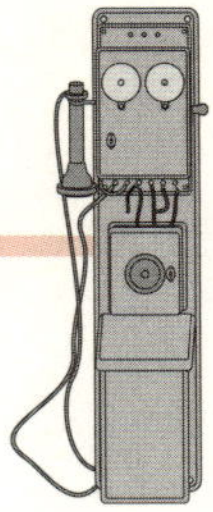

Italian Chicken Soup

1 chicken, cut up
½ pound ground meat
2 heaping tablespoons grated Parmesan cheese
2 heaping tablespoons bread crumbs
1 or 2 eggs
Salt, pepper, and parsley to taste
1 or 2 celery stalks with leaves
2–3 carrots
1–2 onions
1 (8-ounce) can tomato sauce or several ripe tomatoes, mashed

Put chicken in large 5-quart kettle in water that has come to a boil. Salt to taste. Skim top of soup as it cooks.

Form 1-inch meatballs from mixture of ground meat, cheese, bread crumbs, eggs, and seasonings. Put meatballs into boiling soup. Add veggies, diced or sliced, adding any other veggies you like. Add tomato sauce; cook about an hour until white meat of chicken is done and veggies are tender. Chicken may be removed from soup and served in parts or boned and return to soup. Serve over cooked rice or noodles. (Rice or noodles may be partially cooked, drained, then finished in hot soup.) Serves 8–10.

Cindy Morrison (Recipes to Remember)

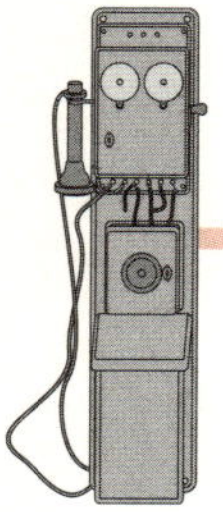

Chicken Rice Soup

1½ cups very finely chopped celery
⅓ cup very finely chopped onion
4 cups water
1 cup finely chopped, cooked, boned chicken
1 chicken bouillon cube, dissolved in 1 cup hot water
1 cup Minute Rice
Dash of black pepper, red pepper, salt
1 heaping tablespoon flour, mixed with 1 cup cold water
1 tablespoon finely mashed pimento

Boil celery and onion in water until tender; leave covered and turn off heat. Add chicken, bouillon, and rice. Add pepper, red pepper, and salt. Stir in flour/water mixture to thicken. Add mashed pimento; stir well. Serves 4–6.

Leann Hall (Cookins for Gulf Coast Council / Blue)

Chicken Noodle Soup

1 whole chicken, cut up
1 (8- to 10-ounce) package small egg noodles
1 cup sliced carrots
1 cup frozen peas
1 (10¾-ounce) can cream of mushroom soup
1 (10¾-ounce) can cream of celery soup
½ block Velveeta, cubed

In large pot, boil chicken in enough water to cover 30–45 minutes, or until chicken is falling off the bone. Remove chicken from water; keep 4 cups broth. Strain broth and bring back to a boil; add noodles, then carrots, and peas during last 5 minutes of cooking noodles. Debone chicken and cut into bite-size pieces. When noodles are done, add chicken, soups, and Velveeta; heat thoroughly, until all cheese is melted and soups are dissolved. Serves 8–10.

Michelle Stuyvesant (Recipes to Remember)

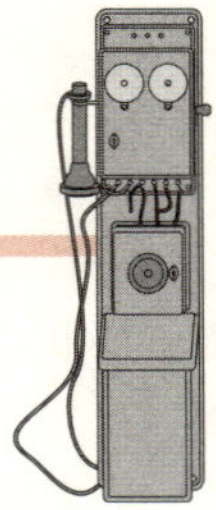

Homemade Soup

1½–2 pounds boneless stew meat
1 soup bone
1 large onion, coarsely chopped
Salt and pepper to taste
3 or 4 large potatoes, peeled, cubed
1 small package carrots, scraped, sliced
1 (20-ounce) can tomatoes
1 (8-ounce) can tomato sauce
1 small head cabbage, chopped
1 (15-ounce) can whole-kernel corn, drained
1 (15-ounce) can English peas, drained
1 (15-ounce) can green beans, drained

Place stew meat, soup bone, onion, and seasoning in water to cover. Cook for 1 hour, adding more water, if needed.

Add potatoes, carrots, tomatoes, tomato sauce, and cabbage; cook till vegetables are tender. Add remaining ingredients and cook 20–25 minutes. Serve with hot cornbread.

Doris Owens (Cookins for Gulf Coast Council / Red)

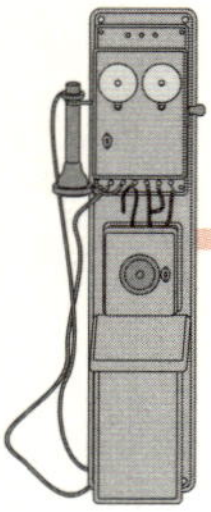

Cauliflower Soup

1 head cauliflower, cut into bite-size pieces
Water
2 chicken bouillon cubes
3 tablespoons butter
3 tablespoons all-purpose flour
1 (12-ounce) can evaporated milk
2 cups diced cooked chicken
Salt and pepper to taste
Cubed Swiss cheese for garnish
Parmesan cheese for garnish

Place cauliflower in a 4-quart pot and add water so that cauliflower is covered by 1 inch. Add chicken bouillon and simmer gently until cauliflower is barely tender.

Melt butter in saucepan and add flour. Cook over medium heat until flour is incorporated; do not allow to brown. Add 1 cup broth from the cauliflower, little by little, until a thick gravy forms. Use a fork or whisk to prevent lumps. Stir gravy and evaporated milk into cauliflower. Add diced chicken to soup and bring to a simmer so that the soup will thicken slightly. Do not allow soup to boil too long or it will scorch. Add salt and pepper to taste. Serve with a couple of cubes of Swiss cheese and a sprinkle of Parmesan. Serves 4–6.

Isabell Montenegro (Our Favorite Recipes)r

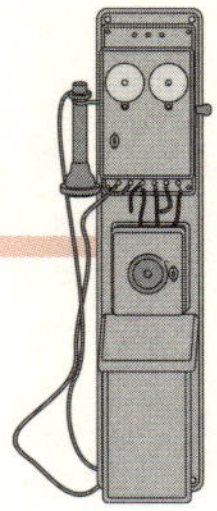

Chunky Cheese Soup

2 medium baking potatoes, micro-baked
6 slices bacon
1 (12-ounce) can beer
1 (14-ounce) can chicken broth
1 teaspoon Worcestershire
½ cup half-and-half
¼ cup cornstarch
1 (16-ounce) jar processed cheese spread
1 cup milk
¼ teaspoon ground red pepper
½ cup shredded sharp Cheddar cheese
Chopped fresh chives

Peel potatoes and cut into chunks; set aside. Cook bacon in microwave dish 5–7 minutes, or until crisp; drain; crumble; set aside. Combine beer, broth, and Worcestershire in 3-quart casserole. Microwave on HIGH 3–4 minutes, or until hot. Combine half-and-half and cornstarch; stir well; add mixture, cheese spread, milk, and red pepper to beer mixture; stir well. Cover and microwave at MEDIUM-HIGH 4 minutes. Serve in individual serving bowls, adding reserved crumbled bacon, shredded Cheddar, and chives on top. Makes 8 cups.

(Country Favorites)

Canadian Cheese Soup

¾ cup chopped celery
¾ cup chopped green bell pepper
¾ cup chopped onion
¾ cup chopped carrots
4 tablespoons plus ½ cup butter, divided
3 cups chicken stock, divided
6 tablespoons all-purpose flour
1 quart milk or half-and-half
1 teaspoon salt
3 cups grated cheese

Sauté vegetables in 4 tablespoons butter; add 1 cup chicken stock and cook to crunchy stage. Add remaining stock and bring to a boil.

Make cream sauce of ½ cup butter, flour, milk, and salt; add cheese and vegetable mixture. Heat, but do not boil. Serves 4.

Susan Rea (Cookins for Gulf Coast Council / Red)

Frijoles `a la Charra

4 cups pinto beans
1 garlic pod, the size of half dollar, outer edges peeled and left intact
¾ cup salt pork, diced
1 medium-size onion, chopped
1 medium-size tomato, chopped
1 small bunch cilantro leaves, chopped
1 (8-ounce) can Herdez red salsa, or 1 cup medium flavor picante
1 heaping tablespoon salt

In 5-quart slow cooker, place beans, garlic, and salt pork in water 2 inches from top. Cook until tender. Remove garlic pod. Add remaining ingredients and cook for 1 hour. Do not stir unless absolutely necessary during cooking process. The liquid should remain clear.

Anita Vela (Our Favorite Recipes)

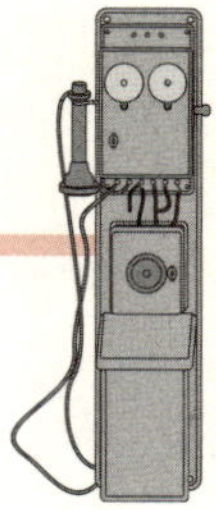

Corn Chowder

6 slices bacon, cut crosswise into julienne strips
1 medium onion, chopped
¼ pound small mushrooms, sliced
1 large potato, diced
½ cup water
1 teaspoon salt
2 cups milk
1 (15-ounce) can cream-style corn
1 (10¾-ounce) can cream of mushroom soup
1 (4-ounce) can chopped green chiles

Cook bacon in large saucepan until crisp; drain. Pour fat from pan into cup, then spoon 3 teaspoons of fat back into pan. Stir-fry onion, mushrooms, and potato in fat about 5 minutes, or until golden. Stir in water, cover, and simmer 15 minutes, or until potatoes are tender. Add salt, milk, corn, and soup. Bring to just boiling; stir in chiles. Lower heat and simmer 5 minutes. Top each serving with bacon.

Cindy Morrison (Recipes to Remember)

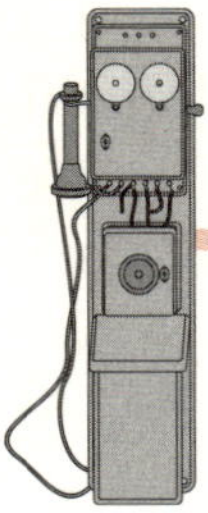

Galveston Gumbo

2 cups sliced fresh okra, or 1 (10-ounce) package frozen, sliced okra
⅓ cup shortening, melted
⅔ cup chopped green onions and tops
3 cloves garlic, finely chopped
1½ teaspoons salt
½ teaspoon pepper
1 pound raw frozen shrimp, peeled, deveined, thawed
2 cups hot water
1 cup canned tomatoes, chopped
2 whole bay leaves
6 drops Tabasco
1½ cups cooked rice

Sauté okra in shortening about 10 minutes, or until okra appears dry, stirring constantly. Add onions, garlic, salt, pepper, and shrimp. Cook about 5 minutes. Add water, tomatoes, and bay leaves; cover and simmer 20 minutes. Remove bay leaves; add Tabasco. Place ¼ cup rice in bottom of 6 soup bowls; fill with gumbo. Serves 6.

Ora Nell Weber (Cookins for Gulf Coast Council / Blue)

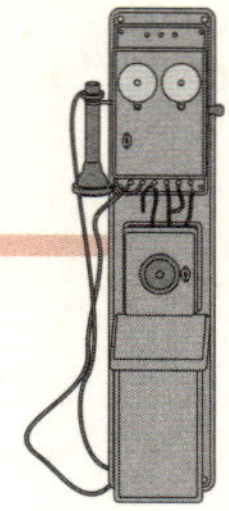

Seafood Gumbo

1 stick margarine
1 cup chopped onions
½ cup chopped celery
½ cup chopped green bell pepper
4 cloves garlic, minced
2 cups chopped okra
3 quarts water
1 tablespoon Worcestershire
4 cleaned crabs and claws, cut in fourths
2 pounds fresh peeled shrimp
½ pound fish fillets, cut in bite-size pieces
½ pint oysters
1 (14½-ounce) can whole tomatoes
Cooked rice
½ cup chopped green onion tops and parsley
Filé

In large Dutch oven, sauté in margarine the onions, celery, green pepper, garlic, and okra for 10 minutes. Add water and Worcestershire; cook 1 hour. Add all other ingredients, except onion tops and parsley, and cook another hour. Serve in soup plate with rice, garnished with onion tops and parsley and a dash of filé. Serves 8.

Mary Jordan (Cookins for Gulf Coast Council / Blue)

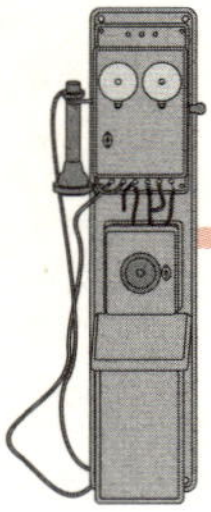

Taco Chili

1 pound ground turkey
1 onion, chopped
2–3 cloves garlic, crushed
6 cups chopped celery
4 fresh tomatoes, chopped (optional)
1 (15-ounce) can kidney or pinto beans, drained
1 (15-ounce) can tomato sauce
1 (4-ounce) can diced green chiles
1 (14½-ounce) can diced tomatoes
1 package taco seasoning
1 package ranch dressing mix
8 teaspoons cumin
1 (16-ounce) package frozen or canned corn, undrained
½ cup water

Brown turkey, onion, and garlic in large skillet. Add celery and cook till tender. Add remaining ingredients; let cook until tender and thick. Serves 6–8.

Betty Hatcher (Our Favorite Recipes)

Chili con Carne

2 pounds beef
2 tablespoons Gebhardt's chili powder
2 cloves garlic, minced
3 tablespoons all-purpose flour
4 tablespoons fat
2 tablespoons chopped suet
1 large onion, chopped
2 teaspoons salt
1½ quarts hot water
1 (20-ounce) can Gebhardt's Mexican-Style Beans (optional)

Use cheaper cut of meat; cut in small chunks. Mix with chili powder, garlic, and flour. Melt fat and suet in deep pot; fry onion until tender; add meat mixture. Cook 15 minutes, then add salt, and gradually pour in hot water. Simmer 45 minutes, or until tender. If chili with beans is desired, add; heat thoroughly. Serves 4–6.

(Country Favorites)

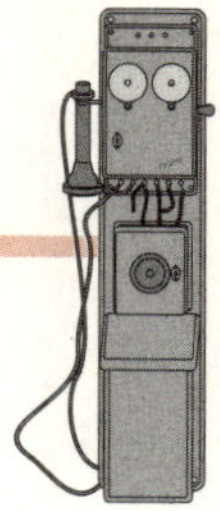

Dale's Chili

4 pounds coarse ground round
3–4 slices bacon
6 heaping tablespoons chili powder
3 tablespoons cocoa, or 3 squares baking chocolate
3 tablespoons ground cumin
2 teaspoons salt
2 teaspoons ground red pepper
1 tablespoon ground cinnamon
2 large onions, chopped
8 cloves garlic, pressed
2 green bell peppers, chopped (optional)
5 cups water
3 beef bouillon cubes
⅓ cup jalapeño juice
2 (14½-ounce) cans diced tomatoes, undrained

Cook beef in large skillet with bacon till done. Stir in dry ingredients, onions, garlic, and bell peppers. Add water, bouillon cubes, jalapeño juice, and tomatoes. Remove bacon. Bring to a boil and simmer 1 hour. Stir often. Serves 12 or more.

Dale Hart (Our Favorite Recipes)

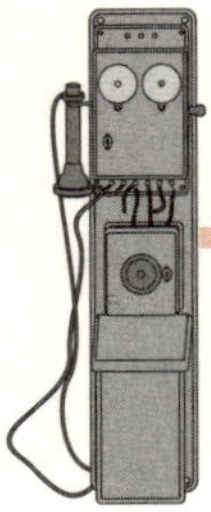

Dinner Pot Chili

2 pounds ground meat
1 medium onion, diced
1 (8-ounce) can tomato sauce
16 ounces water
7 tablespoons chili powder
1½ teaspoons comino
1½ teaspoons oregano
1½ teaspoons salt
1½ teaspoons paprika
1 teaspoon red pepper
4 bay leaves
1 teaspoon thyme
1 clove garlic, minced
5 teaspoons masa trigo flour

In medium kettle, sear meat and onions until meat is grayish color. Add tomato sauce and water. Add remaining ingredients except masa flour. Cover kettle and simmer 15 minutes, or until meat is tender; stir occasionally. Skim off grease. Mix masa flour with warm water into a thick, but flowable mixture, and stir into chili to thicken and to add flavor. Let simmer another 15–20 minutes, then taste for salt and meat tenderness. Add salt to your taste. You now have chili ready to serve. Makes 2 quarts.

Ashland Pioneer Club (Our Favorite Recipes)

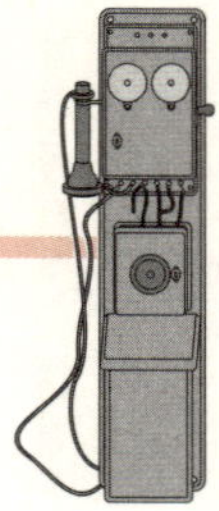

Sambo's Chili

1 pound regular sausage or 1 link sausage, diced
2 pounds thinly sliced steak, diced fine
Fiesta fajita seasoning
1–2 onions, diced
2 packages McCormick chili seasoning
3 tablespoons chili quick
4 beef bouillon cubes
1 (15-ounce) can kidney beans, rinsed
1 (15-ounce) can pinto beans
1 (15-ounce) can red beans
3 long red chile peppers (optional)
1 (8-ounce) can tomato sauce (optional)

Brown sausage; drain. Add steak; season with fajita seasoning and brown. Add onion and sauté 5 minutes. Stir in chili seasoning and chili quick; add beef bouillon and enough water to cover meat 2 inches. Lightly boil, covered, 1–2 hours. Add beans.

Add red chiles and tomato sauce, if using. Cook an additional hour at low boil.

Samuel Shores (Recipes to Remember)

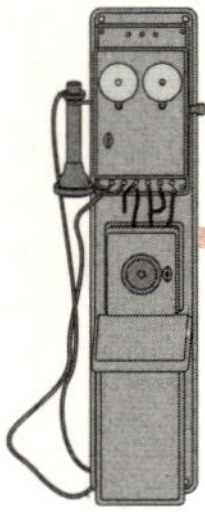

Texas Beef Stew

2 pounds round steak
½ cup water
½ cup vinegar
¼ cup ketchup
1 tablespoon Worcestershire
Dash of Tabasco
2 teaspoons salt
1 teaspoon black pepper
1 teaspoon chili powder
1 clove garlic, minced
2 bay leaves
2 large onions, sliced

Cut steak in crosswise strips, 1 inch wide. Mix water and vinegar with ketchup and other seasonings; pour over meat. Let stand several hours, turning meat occasionally. Lift meat from liquid, saving mixture. Place meat in pan, top with sliced onions, and add ½ of the reserved vinegar mixture. Cover; simmer gently over low heat 1½–2 hours, adding vinegar mixture as required to keep liquid about ½ inch deep in pan. Remove meat and onions to hot platter; strain liquid, then boil hard 3–4 minutes; pour over meat and serve while hot. Serves 6.

(Country Favorites)

Cowboy Stew

1 pound lean hamburger meat
1 onion, chopped
1 green bell pepper, chopped
3 potatoes, peeled, cubed
2 cups water
Salt, pepper, and garlic powder to taste

Brown meat with onion and bell pepper; add potatoes and water. Add salt, pepper, and garlic powder to taste; simmer about 25 minutes or till potatoes are tender. Good over rice. Serves 4.

Marty Horn (Cookins for Gulf Coast Council / Red)

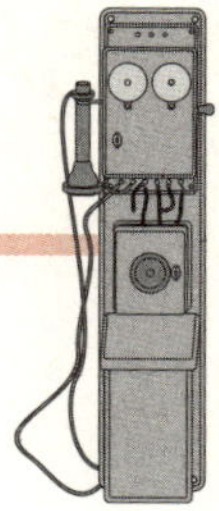

Hearty Beef Stew

½ cup all-purpose flour
1 teaspoon salt and pepper
1 tablespoon Fiesta fajita seasoning
2 pounds beef stew meat, cubed
4 tablespoons vegetable oil
1 (8-ounce) package sliced mushrooms
4 beef bouillon cubes
McCormick beef stew mix
4 large potatoes, cut in 1- to 2-inch cubes
2 cups sliced celery
½ small head cabbage, chopped
2 cups sliced squash (yellow or zucchini)
1 onion, chopped
1 green bell pepper, chopped
½ cup chopped cilantro
½ cup sliced carrots
1 bay leaf
1 teaspoon garlic salt
1 teaspoon oregano
Salt to taste

Mix flour, salt, pepper, and fajita seasoning in a large mixing bowl or gallon-size ziplock bag. Add stew meat and coat completely. Heat oil in 6-quart pot; brown meat. Add mushrooms and bouillon cubes; stir in stew mix. Add enough water to cover meat 2 inches; simmer on medium heat 30 minutes. Add remaining ingredients. Cover and simmer on medium heat 2 hours, stirring occasionally to prevent sticking. Salt to taste. Serves 8.

Samuel Shores (Recipes to Remember)

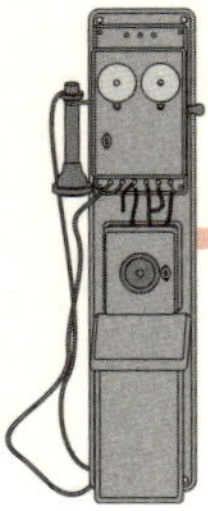

Calabaza con Puerco

(Pork and Squash Stew)

2 pounds pork steak, cubed
Salt and pepper to taste
2 pounds zucchini squash, sliced
1 (15-ounce) can whole-kernel corn, drained
1 (8-ounce) can tomato sauce
3 cloves garlic, crushed
¼ teaspoon powdered comino
8 ounces water
Cooked rice

In large skillet or Dutch oven, cook pork until browned; salt and pepper while browning. Add zucchini, corn, tomato sauce, garlic, comino, and water. Stir together and simmer until squash is cooked, about 15 minutes over moderate heat. Serve over rice. Makes 4 servings.

Juanita Herrera (Cookins for Gulf Coast Council / Red)

Salads

1892
Desk Set

The first common battery arrangement came into play in the 1890s, providing electricity to all telephones controlled by the central office. Previously, each customer's telephone needed its own battery to power the transmitter. The innovation of the common battery changed telephone design. The big, bulky wall sets with wet batteries providing power and cranks to signal the operator could now be replaced with sleek desk sets. Since the crank and batteries were no longer required, the subset could be mounted on the wall and out of the way. When you wanted to place a call, you would simply pick up the receiver and wait for the operator. When you finished your call, you could just hang up. Long-distance calling reached a major milestone in 1892, when telephone service between New York and Chicago began. This 950–mile circuit was the longest line possible with the existing technology.

Main Dish Salad

2 cups cooked beef strips or cubes
1 (20-ounce) can kidney beans, drained
1 cup chopped celery
¼ cup chopped onion
2 hard-cooked eggs, chopped
2 tablespoons sliced sweet pickles
¼ cup mayonnaise
1 tablespoon chili sauce
1 teaspoon salt
1 head lettuce

Combine beef, beans, celery, onion, eggs, pickles, mayonnaise, chili sauce, and salt in a bowl; toss lightly. Cover and chill 30 minutes. Serve in lettuce cups. Makes 4–6 servings.

Donna Wilcox (Cookins for Gulf Coast Council / Red)

Peggy's Spinach Salad

1 pound fresh tender spinach, washed, dried, torn
½ pound bacon, fried crisp, crumbled
1 (15-ounce) can bean sprouts, drained
1 (8-ounce) can sliced water chestnuts, drained
5 hard-boiled eggs, sliced
1 bunch green onions, sliced
½ pound fresh mushrooms, sliced

Combine all ingredients in salad bowl.

DRESSING:

½ cup sugar
1 cup oil
½ cup ketchup
¼ cup vinegar
1 teaspoon Worcestershire

Whirl in blender. Pour over salad and toss just before serving. Serves 6–8.

Mary Jordan (Cookins for Gulf Coast Council / Blue)

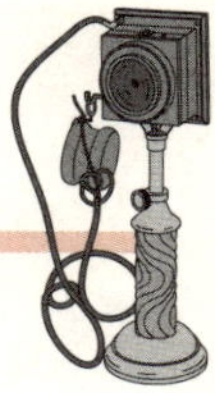

Mexican Chef Salad

1½–2 pounds ground meat
1 (15-ounce) can kidney beans
Salt and pepper to taste
½ onion, chopped
2–3 avocados, peeled, chopped
1 (4-ounce) package shredded Cheddar cheese
½ head lettuce, torn
1 tomato, cubed
Picante sauce
Thousand Island salad dressing
1 bag Doritos

Brown ground meat; drain. Add kidney beans; season to taste. Place chopped onion, avocados, and grated cheese in separate bowls. Mix lettuce and tomato together. Place meat-bean mixture on plate; top with lettuce and tomato salad. Add onion, avocados, and cheese; top with picante sauce, followed by Thousand Island dressing. Serve with Doritos. Serves 4–6.

Joyce Abraham (Cookins for Gulf Coast Council / Red)

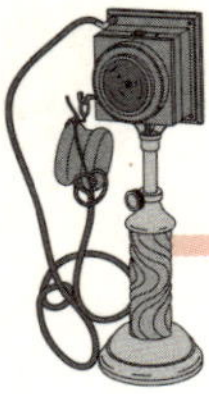

Crunchy Cabbage Salad

1 (3-ounce) package lime gelatin
1 cup boiling water
2 teaspoons white vinegar
1 cup mayonnaise
½ cup whipping cream
1½ cups shredded cabbage
1½ teaspoons finely chopped onion
Lettuce leaves

Combine gelatin and boiling water; stir 2 minutes, or until gelatin dissolves; stir in vinegar. Cover and chill to consistency of unbeaten egg white. Fold in mayonnaise, whipping cream, cabbage, and onion. Pour mixture into a lightly oiled 4-cup mold and cover with aluminum foil; chill until firm. Unmold onto a lettuce-lined plate. Serves 4–6.

(Country Favorites)

Confetti Slaw

1 medium head green cabbage, shredded
1 small head red cabbage, shredded
1 green bell pepper, shredded
4 carrots, scraped, shredded
10 radishes, shredded
20 stuffed green olives, sliced
Salt and pepper to taste
¾ cup white vinegar
1½ cups oil
2 tablespoons sugar
2 teaspoons celery seeds
1½ cups mayonnaise

Combine vegetables with olives. Mix salt, pepper, vinegar, oil, sugar, and celery seeds; shake to mix well. Pour over vegetables. Add mayonnaise and toss well. Cover and refrigerate; chill several hours before serving. May be prepared the day before serving. Serves 15.

Donna Wilcox (Cookins for Gulf Coast Council / Red)

Fennel-Lime Coleslaw

½ cup mayonnaise
¼ cup chopped fresh parsley
3 tablespoons lime juice
2 tablespoons cider vinegar
1 tablespoon sugar
¼ teaspoon garlic powder
4 cups fresh cut green cabbage
2 cups thinly sliced red cabbage
½ bulb fennel
5 large radishes

In large bowl, combine mayonnaise, parsley, lime juice, vinegar, sugar, and garlic powder. Add green and red cabbage; stir until cabbage is well coated with dressing. Trim stalks off fennel and discard; cut fennel in half lengthwise. Cut each piece crosswise into thin slices. Cut radishes in halves through root end. Cut each half crosswise into slices about ¼ inch thick. Add fennel and radish slices to bowl with coleslaw; toss until well coated with dressing. Cover bowl; refrigerate at least 2 hours before serving.

(Recipes to Remember)

In 1877, Bell Telephone Company was formed to operate local telephone exchange operation, installing the first city exchange in Hartford, Connecticut.

Great Veggie Salad

It's ideal to make the salad the night before so the dressing will soak into veggies; however, it can be served the same day you make it.

2 cups fresh mushrooms
1 bunch broccoli florets
Few slices red onion, separated
1 head cauliflower
2 zucchini
2 yellow squash
2 cups sliced tomatoes
1 (14-ounce) jar Caesar dressing

Cut all vegetables into small bite-size pieces. Pour dressing over and mix well. Makes a lot.

Judy Jaksik (Our Favorite Recipes)

Green Bean Salad

1 (15-ounce) can French-style green beans, drained
1 (15-ounce) can English peas, drained
1 (4-ounce) jar chopped pimentos
1 medium onion, chopped
1 green bell pepper, chopped
4 stalks celery, chopped

Combine all ingredients in glass bowl.

DRESSING:

¾ cup sugar
½ cup vinegar
¼ cup corn oil
1 tablespoon salt

Combine ingredients; pour over vegetables and marinate overnight. Drain before serving. Serves 6–8.

Mabel Ephran (Cookins for Gulf Coast Council / Blue)

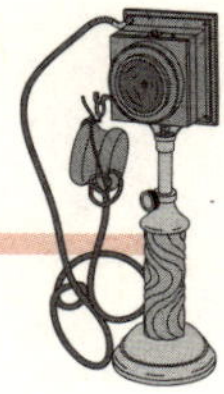

Roasted Corn and Black Bean Salad

1 (1-pound) package frozen corn
1–2 tablespoons oil
1 cup chopped cilantro
3 plump tomatoes, chopped
2 jalapeño peppers, finely chopped
½ cup chopped red onion
1 red bell pepper, chopped
2 teaspoons minced garlic
2 (15-ounce) cans black beans, drained, rinsed
2 large avocados, chopped (optional)

Preheat oven to 450°. Combine corn and oil in baking dish. Bake 18–22 minutes, or until corn is roasted; set aside. Combine remaining ingredients and add cool roasted corn; mix well. Pour Dressing over mixture. May be served with tortilla chips as a dip, or as a side dish.

DRESSING:

1 tablespoon salt
¾ cup cumin
6 tablespoons lime juice
5 tablespoons oil
2 tablespoons cider vinegar

Combine ingredients in small jar and shake until well blended.

Gladys Haecker (Our Favorite Recipes)

Martha's Summer Special

Salad is better after 24 hours. Great with barbecue and beans.

3 medium cucumbers, peeled, sliced
3 tomatoes, chunked
1 green bell pepper, chopped or thinly sliced
1 red onion, sliced
½–¾ cup vinegar
¾ cup sugar
⅓ cup oil

Prepare vegetables; mix vinegar, sugar, and oil and cover vegetables. Marinate overnight before serving. Serves 2–4.

Martha Safford (Our Favorite Recipes)

Cornbread Salad

2 (7-ounce) packages yellow cornbread mix
1 large green bell pepper, finely chopped
1 large onion, finely chopped
1 large tomato, chopped
2 stalks celery, chopped
1 (2-ounce) jar chopped pimento
½ cup chopped pecans
1 teaspoon salt
1 pint Miracle Whip salad dressing

Cook cornbread mix as directed on package; cool and crumble. Combine all ingredients, folding in Miracle Whip last. Chill. Serves 8–10.

(Country Favorites)

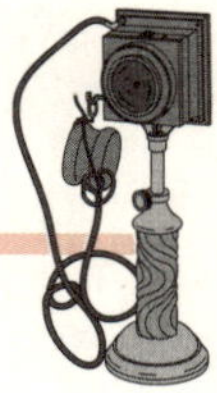

Guacamole Salad

2 avocados, peeled
2 hard-cooked eggs, chopped
6 stuffed olives, sliced
½ teaspoon chili powder
3 small tomatoes, diced
1 medium onion, minced
¼ cup French dressing
Salt to taste
Gebhardt's chili powder to taste
Lettuce leaves
Crisp bacon for garnish

Combine avocados, eggs, olives, chili powder, tomatoes, onion, and French dressing. Season to taste with salt and chili powder. Serve on crisp lettuce leaves with additional French dressing. Garnish with crisp bacon. Serves 4.

(Country Favorites)

Johnson Family Potato Salad

6 potatoes, peeled
1 bunch green onions, white parts only
2 dill pickles
4 hard-boiled eggs
1 (2-ounce) jar chopped pimentos, drained
¼ cup prepared mustard
1½–2 cups Miracle Whip salad dressing
Salt and pepper to taste

In large pot, boil potatoes until tender. While potatoes are boiling, dice onions, pickles, and eggs; set aside. Drain and mash potatoes to desired consistency. In large bowl, mix potatoes, onions, pickles, eggs, mustard, and Miracle Whip until all ingredients are incorporated. Add salt and pepper to taste. Serves 8–10.

Michelle Stuyvesant (Recipes to Remember)

Dill Salmon Pasta Salad

1½ cups tri-colored spiral pasta
½ cup sour cream
½ cup mayonnaise
¼ cup chopped green bell pepper
¼ cup chopped red bell pepper
1½ tablespoons minced fresh dill, or 1½ teaspoons dill weed
1 (7-ounce) can salmon, drained, bones and skin removed
Mixed salad greens

Cook pasta according to package directions. Combine next 5 ingredients in a bowl. Drain and rinse pasta in cold water; add to sour cream mixture. Stir in salmon. Cover and refrigerate. Serve over salad greens. Serves 4.

Louise Kosub (Our Favorite Recipes)

Shrimp Salad

2 pounds, cooked, cleaned shrimp
1 medium onion, finely chopped
½ cup chopped celery
½ cup chopped dill pickle
3 hard-boiled eggs, chopped
1 small package elbow macaroni
Salt, pepper, onion salt, and garlic salt to taste
2 cups mayonnaise (add a little oil if not moist enough)

Mix all ingredients and serve on lettuce leaves. Serves 8–10.

Marty Martorell (Cookins for Gulf Coast Council / Blue)

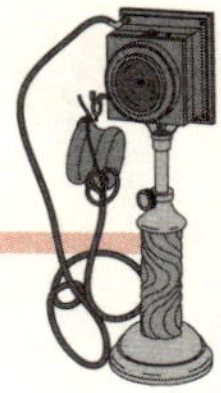

Sea Island Tuna Salad

1 (7-ounce) package Creamettes macaroni
½ cup mayonnaise
½ cup sour cream
½ teaspoon celery seeds
½ teaspoon onion salt
1 (7-ounce) can tuna, drained
1 (17-ounce) can sweet peas, drained
¾ cup diced mild Cheddar cheese
2 tablespoons minced green bell pepper
1 tablespoon diced pimento

Cook macaroni according to package directions; drain. Stir in mayonnaise; blend with sour cream and seasonings. Gently stir in tuna, sweet peas, and remaining ingredients. Makes 6–8 servings.

Johnnie Johnson (Cookins for Gulf Coast Council / Red)

Crab Louie

1½ pounds crabmeat
6 hard-cooked eggs, sliced
4 tomatoes, cut in wedges
1 avocado, sliced
Crisp lettuce
1 cup mayonnaise
½ cup heavy cream
4 tablespoons chili sauce
1 teaspoon Worcestershire
1 teaspoon horseradish
1 teaspoon minced parsley
1 green bell pepper, chopped
3 stuffed olives, chopped
1 small onion, chopped
Salt and pepper to taste

Arrange crab, egg slices, tomato wedges, and avocado slices in a bed of crisp lettuce. Combine remaining ingredients; pour over salad and serve cold. Serves 8.

Glen J. Adams (Cookins for Gulf Coast Council / Red)

Tomato/Mozzarella Salad

½ cup mayonnaise
2 tablespoons oil
1 teaspoon salt
½ teaspoon sugar
3 tablespoons white wine vinegar
2 tablespoons milk
1 teaspoon fresh minced basil, or ¼ teaspoon dried basil
Fresh basil or spinach leaves
3 medium tomatoes, sliced
1 medium cucumber, sliced
1 (8-ounce) package mozzarella cheese, sliced

Mix first 7 ingredients with fork or wire whisk for dressing; set aside. Line large platter with basil or spinach leaves. Arrange alternating slices of tomato, cucumber, and mozzarella cheese, overlapping slices. Spoon dressing over vegetables and cheese to serve. Makes 8 servings.

Frances Lawrence (Cookins for Gulf Coast Council / Red)

Cool Cucumber Salad

1 large cucumber, peeled, sliced
1 large sweet onion, sliced thin
1 (8-ounce) container sour cream
¼ cup milk
Salt and pepper to taste

Add cucumber and onion to sour cream, milk, and salt and pepper. Allow to refrigerate overnight for better flavor.

(Country Favorites)

Pretzel Surprise

Unsalted pretzels
½ cup plus 2 tablespoons sugar, divided
1½ sticks butter
1 (6-ounce) box strawberry Jell-O
2 (10-ounce) cartons frozen strawberries
2 cups boiling water
1 (8-ounce) package cream cheese, softened
1 (8-ounce) carton Cool Whip

Break pretzels; line bottom of 9x13-inch pan. Melt 2 tablespoons sugar with butter; pour over pretzels. Bake at 350° approximately 10 minutes; remove to cool.

Blend Jell-O, strawberries, and boiling water together. Put in refrigerator to set, about 1 hour.

Blend cream cheese, Cool Whip, and ½ cup sugar in mixer. To assemble, pour cream cheese mixture over cooled pretzels. Pour Jell-O mixture over cream cheese mixture. Cut into squares to serve.

Ofe Gonzales (Recipes to Remember)

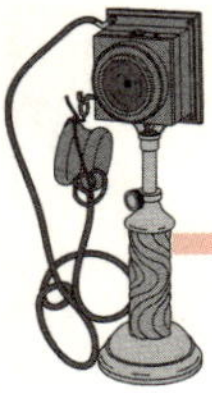

Angel Hash Salad

1 (15-ounce) can crushed pineapple, drain, reserve juice
2 (15-ounce) cans fruit cocktail, drain, reserve juice
2 tablespoons all-purpose flour
¼ cup sugar
2 egg yolks
1 cup reserved juices from fruits
1 cup whipped cream or Cool Whip
¼ cup chopped pecans
2 cups mini marshmallows

Combine fruits in glass bowl; set aside. In saucepan, combine flour, sugar, egg yolks, and reserved juices; cook, stirring until thick; cool completely. When cold, fold in whipped cream, pecans, and marshmallows. Combine with fruit; let sit overnight in refrigerator. Serves 4–6.

(Cookins for Gulf Coast Council / Blue)

Coca-Cola Salad

2 (3-ounce) packages black cherry Jell-O (or 1 cherry and 1 raspberry)
1½ cups hot liquid (can be juice from fruits)
1 (20-ounce) can sour pitted cherries, drained
1 (15-ounce) can crushed pineapple, drained
1 cup chopped nuts
16 ounces Coca-Cola

Dissolve Jell-O in hot liquid; cool. Add fruit and nuts. Cool well; add Coca-Cola. Let set up; serve on lettuce leaves. Serves 6–8.

Elfreida Schreiber (Cookins for Gulf Coast Council / Blue)

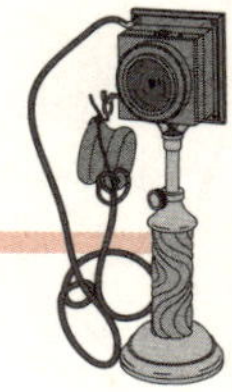

Cranberries Waldorf

Ground fresh cranberries lend a pleasant tartness to this frothy pink salad. A real buffet special.

2 cups raw cranberries
3 cups miniature marshmallows
¾ cup sugar
2 cups diced, unpared tart apples
½ cup seedless green grapes
½ cup broken California walnuts
¼ teaspoon salt
1 cup whipping cream, whipped

Grind cranberries and combine with marshmallows and sugar; cover and chill overnight.

Add apples, grapes, walnuts, and salt. Fold in whipped cream; chill. Serve in large bowl or individual lettuce cups. Garnish with clusters of green and red grapes, if desired. Makes 8–10 servings.

Bert Atwood (Cookins for Gulf Coast Council / Blue)

Green Tomato Relish

1 gallon tender green tomatoes, chopped
½ gallon green bell peppers, chopped
8 pods hot green peppers, chopped
½ gallon onions, chopped
3 pints vinegar
4 tablespoons salt
5 cups sugar
1 teaspoon black pepper
2 teaspoons pickling spices (tied in cloth)

Mix chopped vegetables in very large kettle. Combine vinegar, salt, sugar, pepper, and spices. Pour mixture over vegetables in kettle; heat to boiling. Remove spice bag. Immediately begin filling hot jars; seal. Allow relish to ripen at least a week before opening.

Audrey Morgan (Cookins for Gulf Coast Council / Blue)

Frosted Fruit Mold

1 (3-ounce) package lime Jell-O
1 cup boiling water
7 ounces 7-Up
1 (8-ounce) can crushed pineapple, drain, reserve juice
1 banana, sliced
¼ cup sugar
1 tablespoon flour
1 egg, slightly beaten
½ cup Cool Whip or whipped cream
¼ cup shredded sharp Cheddar cheese
2 tablespoons grated Parmesan cheese

Dissolve Jell-O in boiling water; cool; add 7-Up. Chill until partially set. Fold pineapple and banana into Jell-O; turn into 9x9-inch pan; chill till firm.

Combine sugar and flour in saucepan; stir in reserved pineapple juice and egg. Cook and stir over low heat until thickened. Chill. Fold Cool Whip or whipped cream into egg mixture. Spread over firm Jell-O. Serves 6–9.

Willia M. Arline (Cookins for Gulf Coast Council / Blue)

Vegetables

1919
Candlestick

The first dial telephone exchange is credited to Almon B. Strowger who introduced it in LaPorte, Indiana, in 1892. However, it was many years before switching equipment was sufficiently developed to permit dial installation in larger cities. The advent of the vacuum tube amplifier (or repeater) made lines of any length feasible. With repeaters in the line, transcontinental telephone service opened in 1915. Dial service was coming in strongly, and customers could now dial out themselves, with no need to go through an operator. The first dial phones were candlestick phones. To place a call, you lifted the receiver, waited for dial tone, then dialed. The dial tone was a much lower pitched tone than what we hear today. If the switching equipment was busy, dial tone might take several seconds to come on.

Baked Corn Casserole

1 (17-ounce) can cream-style corn
1 (17-ounce) can whole-kernel corn
1 large onion, chopped
1 (2-ounce) jar chopped pimentos
⅔ cup milk
1 egg, beaten
1 cup cracker crumbs
¼ cup butter, melted
Salt, pepper, and red pepper to taste

Mix all ingredients; pour into greased baking dish. Bake at 350° for 1 hour.

Billy and Clara Cash (Our Favorite Recipes)

Baked Corn

3 cups or 2 (9-ounce) packages frozen corn, cooked
1 (6-ounce) can evaporated milk
1 egg, beaten
2 teaspoons minced onion
1 cup grated Swiss cheese, divided
Salt and pepper to taste
1 cup bread crumbs
½ stick margarine, melted

Mix corn, milk, egg, onion, ¾ cup cheese, and seasonings. Place in greased baking dish. Combine bread crumbs, margarine, and remaining ¼ cup cheese; sprinkle over top of corn and bake at 350° for 25 minutes. Serves 6–8.

Joyce Abraham (Cookins for Gulf Coast Council / Blue)

Bill's Fried Corn

6 slices bacon
1 bunch green onions, chopped
1 (15-ounce) can cream-style corn
1 (15-ounce) can whole-kernel corn, drained
1 cup (or more) grated cheese

Fry bacon until crisp; drain on paper towel. Sauté green onions in bacon drippings until tender. Add corn and simmer 10 minutes; add cheese and remove from heat. Add bacon crumbles to top of corn for garnish. Serves 6.

Donna Wilcox (Cookins for Gulf Coast Council / Red)

Corn Casserole

1 large onion, chopped
1 large green bell pepper, chopped
1 stick butter
1 (2-ounce) jar chopped pimentos
2 (15-ounce) cans cream-style corn
2 teaspoons sugar
Salt and pepper to taste
1 egg, slightly beaten
1⅓ cups instant rice
1½ cups grated Cheddar cheese
Paprika

Sauté onion and bell pepper in butter. Remove from heat and add remaining ingredients except cheese and paprika. Mix well; pour into buttered 1½-quart casserole. Pat grated cheese and paprika on top. Bake at 350° for 30–35 minutes. Serves 6.

Linda Rape (Cookins for Gulf Coast Council / Red)

Baked Hominy and Cheese Casserole

3 tablespoons butter
6 tablespoons all-purpose flour
1 teaspoon salt
⅛ teaspoon pepper
½ teaspoon dry mustard
2 cups milk
1 teaspoon Worcestershire
½ teaspoon grated onion
½ pound grated American cheese
2 (20-ounce) cans hominy, drained well
½ cup dry bread crumbs

Melt butter in saucepan and blend in flour, salt, pepper, and mustard. Gradually add milk, and cook over low heat until thick, stirring constantly. Stir in Worcestershire, onion, and cheese. Place hominy in greased 1½-quart casserole and pour cheese sauce over. Sprinkle crumbs on top. Bake in 350° oven for 30 minutes. Makes 6 servings.

Donna Wilcox (Cookins for Gulf Coast Council / Red)

Creole Green Beans

6 slices bacon
2 (16-ounce) cans French-style green beans, drained
1 (16-ounce) can seasoned stewed tomatoes
Salt and pepper to taste

Cook bacon; drain; reserve drippings. Place beans and tomatoes in baking dish. Season with salt and pepper and 3–4 tablespoons bacon drippings. Crumble bacon on top. Cook, uncovered, at 350° for 30 minutes.

(Country Favorites)

Green Beans Oregano

3 cups green beans
4 slices bacon, fried crisp, divided
1 (10¾-ounce) can condensed cream of mushroom soup
1 (4-ounce) can sliced mushrooms
1 envelope onion soup mix
¼ teaspoon oregano

Cook beans until barely done. Mix with remaining ingredients; save 2 slices bacon for garnish. Refrigerate overnight to blend flavors.

Bake in 1½-quart casserole at 350° for 30–40 minutes. Serves 6.

Johnnie Johnson (Cookins for Gulf Coast Council / Red)

Quick Baked Beans

Few pieces crispy fried bacon, crumbled
2 (16-ounce) cans pork and beans
1 tablespoon vinegar
2 tablespoons ketchup
¼ teaspoon dry mustard
1 tablespoon chopped onion
1 tablespoon brown sugar
½ cup syrup

Heat oven to 350°. Mix all ingredients and put in 1-quart casserole. Bake about 1 hour. Serves 6.

Cindy Spears (Cookins for Gulf Coast Council / Red)

Fantastic Baked Beans

6 slices bacon, cut in pieces
1 onion, sliced
2 (16-ounce) cans pork and beans, divided
½–¾ cup brown sugar
1 teaspoon dry mustard
½ cup ketchup
1 jalapeño pepper, chopped (optional)

Cook bacon in frying pan to render fat; remove bacon. Sauté onion in pan drippings until clear; remove; drain grease. Put 1 can beans in casserole dish. Combine sugar and mustard; sprinkle half over beans. Put half the onions and bacon over beans. Top with remaining can of beans and remaining sugar, mustard, onions, bacon, ketchup, and jalapeño, if desired. Bake uncovered for 2½ hours at 325°.

Gloria Peveto De Leon/Les Martin (Our Favorite Recipes)

Sauce for Broccoli

2 tablespoons butter
2 tablespoons olive oil
1½ teaspoons Worcestershire
1 tablespoon vinegar
Red pepper to taste
Salt and pepper to taste
1 teaspoon mustard

Mix all ingredients; heat till butter melts. Pour over cooked broccoli just before serving.

(Country Favorites)

Broccoli Casserole

Here's a creamy, mouthwatering dish I think you'll like—even if you don't usually relish broccoli.

2 (10-ounce) boxes frozen chopped broccoli
½ cup chopped onion, divided
¼ cup grated sharp Cheddar cheese
1 (10¾-ounce) can cream of mushroom soup
½ cup milk
6 saltine crackers
2 tablespoons butter, melted

Boil broccoli with ¼ cup onion until tender. Drain and place in casserole dish. Mix grated cheese and remaining ¼ cup onion; add soup mixed with milk. Pour mixture over broccoli. Crumble crackers and mix with butter; sprinkle on top of casserole. Bake at 350° for 25–30 minutes, or until browned and bubbly. Makes 6–8 servings.

Gaynell Seidler (Cookins for Gulf Coast Council / Red)

Broccoli and Rice Casserole

½ cup chopped celery
½ cup chopped onion
1 tablespoon butter
1 (10-ounce) package frozen chopped broccoli
1 cup uncooked rice
1 (10¾-ounce) can cream of mushroom soup
1 (10¾-ounce) can cream of chicken soup
1 (8-ounce) jar Cheez Whiz
Salt and pepper to taste

Sauté celery and onion in butter. Cook broccoli according to directions. Cook rice according to directions. Combine soups, Cheez Whiz, seasonings, sautéed vegetables, and broccoli with rice. Pour into lightly greased 1½-quart casserole dish and bake 30–40 minutes at 350°. Serves 4–6.

Margaret Flagg (Cookins for Gulf Coast Council / Blue)

Yellow Squash Casserole

3 tablespoons butter
3–4 summer squash, sliced
1 medium onion, chopped
1 (4-ounce) can chopped green chiles
8–10 saltine crackers, crushed
Salt and pepper to taste
1½ cups shredded Cheddar cheese

In skillet, melt butter over medium-high heat. Sauté squash and onion until crisp-tender. Remove from heat; stir in chiles, crackers, salt and pepper. Spoon into greased 1½-quart casserole. Top with cheese; bake at 350° for 15–20 minutes. Serves 4–6.

(Country Favorites)

Fried Squash

3 large white squash
Salt and pepper to taste
2 eggs, beaten
½ cup milk
2 cups buttered bread crumbs
Oil for frying

Peel and slice squash into thin slices. Salt and pepper to taste. Dip squash into mixture of eggs and milk; roll in bread crumbs and dip in milk a second time. Roll squash in bread crumbs and drop into hot grease until brown, approximately 5 minutes. Serves 4–6.

(Country Favorites)

Cabbage Wedge-Meal-In-One

1 small head cabbage
1 cup chopped onion
1 pound ground beef
¼ cup uncooked rice
2 cups canned tomatoes
1 cup hot water
2 teaspoons salt
¼ teaspoon pepper

Remove tough outer leaves from cabbage; cut into 6–8 wedges. Place in a buttered 3-quart skillet or casserole. Arrange onion, ground beef, and rice between wedges. Combine tomatoes, water, and seasonings; pour over ingredients in skillet; cover and bake at 350° for 1½ hours. Serves 4–6.

Dorothy Tubbe (Cookins for Gulf Coast Council / Red)

Tomato Skillet Cabbage

1 (16-ounce) can tomato wedges, drained, reserve juice
1 teaspoon instant beef bouillon
3 cups shredded green cabbage

In medium skillet, heat tomato juice and bouillon until it dissolves. Stir in cabbage; cover tightly. Cook 3 minutes, stirring occasionally. Stir in tomatoes. Cover; cook until cabbage is crisp-tender and tomatoes are heated through, 3–5 minutes. Serves 4.

(Country Favorites)

An exchange is a practical means of communicating between many people who have telephones. The first known exchange linking two major cities was established between New York and Boston in 1883.

Fried Tomatoes

3 firm, unripened tomatoes
2 cups cornmeal
1 teaspoon salt
½ teaspoon pepper
½ teaspoon paprika
1 tablespoon flour
Oil for frying

Slice tomatoes into thick crosswise slices. Combine all dry ingredients; coat tomatoes with mixture. Fry in hot fat until golden brown. Serves 4–6.

(Country Favorites)

Tomato Delights

6 firm ripe tomatoes
Salt to taste
1 medium green bell pepper, chopped
1 small onion, chopped
¼ cup butter, melted
1 cup shredded Cheddar cheese
1 cup cooked rice
1 egg, well beaten
¼ teaspoon oregano
¼ teaspoon basil
¼ teaspoon salt
4 slices bacon, cooked, crumbled
Chopped parsley

Cut a slice from top of each tomato; scoop out pulp, leaving shells intact; reserve pulp. Sprinkle insides of tomato shells lightly with salt; invert to drain. Chop pulp. Sauté pepper and onion in butter; add remaining ingredients, including tomato pulp; stir well. Spoon into tomato shells and place in a shallow baking dish. Bake at 350° for 25–30 minutes. Garnish with parsley. Makes 6 servings.

(Cookins for Gulf Coast Council / Blue)

Baked or Stuffed Tomatoes

3 tablespoons butter
1 large onion, minced
1 rib celery, minced
1 (20-ounce) can stewed tomatoes
1½ cups bread crumbs
1 teaspoon minced parsley
Cooked shrimp, deviled ham, or diced ham (optional)
¼ stick butter
2–3 slices bacon, chopped

Melt butter in iron skillet with onion and celery; cook over low heat till onions are clear. Add tomatoes and bring to a boil, about 2 minutes. Add bread crumbs, saving some for top, and stir well. Add parsley and shrimp or ham, if desired. Turn into a 1-quart casserole and dot with butter and bacon. Sprinkle top with remaining bread crumbs. Bake at 350° until top is brown. Serves 4.

(Country Favorites)

Baked Eggplant

1 eggplant
¼ stick butter
2 tablespoons all-purpose flour
⅔ cup milk
1 cup grated sharp Cheddar cheese
1 cup cracker crumbs
1 cup diced tomatoes
2 eggs, separated
Pinch of salt

Peel and dice eggplant; cook in a little water over low heat until tender. Make cream sauce with butter, flour, and milk; add cheese and melt over low heat. Drain eggplant; mash. Add cracker crumbs, tomatoes, beaten egg yolks, and salt. Combine with cream sauce; fold in stiffly beaten egg whites. Bake at 350° for 30 minutes. Serves 6.

(Country Favorites)

Cafeteria Eggplant Casserole

So many readers have asked us to reprint the recipe for the type of eggplant casserole that is so popular in many cafeterias.

1 medium–large eggplant, peeled, diced
1½ teaspoons salt, divided
½ cup margarine, divided
1 small onion, chopped
1 small green bell pepper, chopped
1 tablespoon brown sugar
2 tablespoons all-purpose flour
1 (16-ounce) can tomatoes, cut up, with liquid
1 cup cornbread crumbs
Grated yellow cheese

Cook eggplant in small amount of water with ½ teaspoon salt 8–10 minutes until tender; drain well. In saucepan, add half the margarine and sauté onion and green pepper; add remaining margarine. Add sugar, remaining salt, and flour, stirring to blend. Add tomatoes; cook, stirring, 5 minutes. Add cornbread crumbs and eggplant. Pour into greased 1½-quart casserole and bake at 350° for 15 minutes. Top with cheese and bake 10–15 minutes longer. Serves 4–6.

Note: This recipe can easily be increased by adding more eggplant and/or cornbread crumbs, or it can be successfully doubled.

Ora Nell Weber (Cookins for Gulf Coast Council / Blue)

Stuffed Eggplant Moussaka

1 tablespoon all-purpose flour
1 small eggplant, cut in half lengthwise
½ pound ground beef
¼ cup finely chopped onion
¾ teaspoon salt
¼ teaspoon garlic powder
⅛ teaspoon pepper
¼ cup shredded Swiss cheese

Shake flour in (10x16-inch) oven browning bag; place in 8x12-inch baking dish. Scoop out pulp of eggplant, leaving a shell ½ inch thick; dice pulp. Brown ground beef; drain. Add onion, salt, garlic, pepper, and diced eggplant; cover and simmer 15 minutes; stir in cheese. Fill eggplant shells with meat mixture; place in bag and spoon White Wine Sauce over top. Close bag with twist tie; make 6 half-inch slits in top. Preheat oven to 350°. Bake 30 minutes or until eggplant is tender.

WHITE WINE SAUCE:

1 tablespoon butter
1 tablespoon all-purpose flour
½ cup milk
2 tablespoons dry white wine
½ teaspoon salt
⅛ teaspoon pepper
Dash of nutmeg

Melt butter in saucepan over low heat; blend in flour. Stir in milk and wine. Heat to boiling, stirring constantly until mixture thickens, about 1 minute. Stir in spices. Makes abut ½ cup.

Ora Nell Weber (Cookins for Gulf Coast Council / Red)

Savory Grilled Potatoes

½ cup Miracle Whip salad dressing
3 cloves garlic, minced
½ teaspoon paprika
¼ teaspoon each: salt and pepper
3 baking potatoes, cut into ¼-inch slices
1 large onion, sliced

Mix salad dressing and seasonings in bowl till well blended. Stir in potatoes and onion to coat. Divide potato mixture evenly among 6 (12-inch) squares of heavy-duty foil. Seal each to form packet. Place foil packets on grill over medium-hot coals. Grill, covered, 25–30 minutes, or until potatoes are tender. Serves 6.

(Country Favorites)

Golden Crusted Potatoes

3 cups instant mashed potatoes
1½ cups creamed cottage cheese
½ cup sour cream
¼ teaspoon white pepper
4 tablespoons finely chopped green onions
¼ teaspoon nutmeg
4 tablespoons margarine, melted
¾ cup slivered almonds

Prepare instant mashed potatoes in usual way, using less liquid, to make stiff. Combine potatoes, creamed cottage cheese, sour cream, pepper, green onions, and nutmeg. Check to see if more salt is needed. Place in a shallow buttered 1½-quart casserole. Cover top with melted margarine and sprinkle with slivered almonds. Bake at 350° for 20–25 minutes, or until bubbling hot and golden crusted. Serves 6.

Donna Wilcox (Cookins for Gulf Coast Council / Red)

Buffet Scalloped Carrots

12 medium carrots, scraped, sliced
¼ cup butter
1 small onion, minced
¼ cup all-purpose flour
1 teaspoon salt
¼ teaspoon dry mustard
2 cups milk
⅛ teaspoon pepper
¼ teaspoon celery salt
1½ pounds American cheese slices
3 cups buttered bread crumbs

Place carrots in saucepan and cover with water; bring to a boil and cover. Reduce heat and simmer 20 minutes; drain.

Melt butter in a saucepan. Add onion and cook over low heat 2–3 minutes. Stir in flour, salt, and mustard; add milk and cook, stirring until smooth. Add pepper and celery salt. Place ⅓ carrots in 2-quart casserole and add ½ cheese. Repeat layers, ending with carrots. Pour sauce over carrots and top with crumbs. Preheat oven to 350°. Bake 25 minutes, or until crumbs are golden brown. Makes 6–8 servings.

Donna Wilcox (Cookins for Gulf Coast Council / Red)

Zippy Baked Carrots

5–6 cups sliced carrots, cut ¼ inch thick
6 slices Swiss cheese

Blanch carrots until tender-crisp. Layer half the carrots in a greased 2-quart baking pan; cover with half the cheese; repeat layers.

SAUCE:

1 small onion, minced
4 tablespoons butter
3 tablespoons all-purpose flour
1 teaspoon salt
1 teaspoon chili powder
2 cups milk

Sauté onion in butter 2 minutes; blend in flour and seasonings. Cook, stirring 1 minute; add milk all at once; cook, stirring until thickened. Pour Sauce over carrots.

TOPPING:

1 cup soft bread crumbs
2 tablespoons butter, melted
5 strips bacon, cooked, crumbled

Combine bread crumbs and butter; sprinkle over casserole. Top with bacon. Bake at 350° for 25 minutes. Makes 8 servings.

(Country Favorites)

Smothered Okra

2½ pounds cut okra
¾ cup oil
1 pound fresh tomatoes, chopped fine
½ cup chopped green bell pepper
1 onion, chopped
Creole seasoning to taste
3 cloves garlic, finely chopped
1 tablespoon tomato paste

In saucepan over medium heat, smother okra in oil 15 minutes; stirring frequently. Add tomatoes, pepper, onion, seasoning, and garlic. Cook 30 minutes; add tomato paste; blend well; cook 15 minutes longer. Serves 6.

Mary West (Cookins for Gulf Coast Council / Blue)

Asparagus Casserole

1 (10-ounce) can asparagus spears, drained
1 (15-ounce) can English peas, drained
1 (10¾-ounce) can cream of mushroom soup
½ cup milk
1 (8-ounce) package grated Cheddar cheese
Bread crumbs

Place vegetables in greased casserole dish. Mix soup, milk, and cheese together; pour over vegetables. Top with bread crumbs; bake at 350° for 15–20 minutes. Serves 4–6.

Catherine Davis (Cookins for Gulf Coast Council / Blue)

Dave's Favorite Artichokes

2 large artichokes
½ cup butter
¼ cup olive oil
3 cloves garlic, minced
1 tablespoon chopped basil
1 tablespoon chopped thyme
⅓ cup white or red wine
Water

Wash artichokes; cut stem to ¾–1 inch in length. Trim off top 1 inch of leaves, and trim thorns from remainder of leaves. Cut in half and remove choke (the fibrous, hairy center) and the small purple leaves with a spoon (a grapefruit spoon works really well).

In a large skillet over medium heat, melt butter with olive oil. Add garlic, basil, and thyme and heat to simmering. Place artichokes, cut side down, in skillet. Add wine and enough water to bring level to ¾ inch deep. Cover and simmer over low heat ½ hour until stem is tender (should pierce easily with fork).

To serve: Place one of the artichoke halves onto a plate. Pour some of the cooking liquid into a small dish. Pull off the leaves one at a time. Dip in the liquid and scrape meat from leaf with your teeth (you will get more meat the closer you get to the heart). When the entire leaves are gone, cut heart into pieces, dip, and savor.

David Cleland (Recipes to Remember)

Turnip Greens

2 bunches turnip greens
4 cups water
1½ teaspoons sugar
1 teaspoon salt
½ teaspoon pepper
¼ pound salt pork

Wash turnip greens thoroughly. Chop greens into small pieces; put in pot with water (more water may be used, if necessary). Add sugar, salt, pepper, and salt pork. Bring to a brisk boil; reduce heat to medium-low, cover, and cook till tender, about 30 minutes.

(Country Favorites)

Southern Black-Eyed Peas

1 (1-pound) package dried black-eyed peas
2 quarts water
1 onion, chopped
¼ green bell pepper, chopped
1 rib celery, chopped
Ham bone, piece of salt pork, or several slices bacon
Salt and pepper to taste

Wash peas; soak overnight or at least 5–6 hours in fresh, cold water; drain.

Put peas in large pot containing at least 2 quarts fresh water. Add onion, green pepper, celery, and meat. Season to taste with salt and pepper. Cook about 2 hours, or until peas are tender enough to mash easily. Add water as needed while cooking. Serves 8.

(Country Favorites)

Candied Yams

4 medium sweet potatoes
1 cup sugar
Dash of salt
1 teaspoon cinnamon or nutmeg
¾ stick butter
2 slices lemon
1 tablespoon flour
¼ cup water

Peel and cut potatoes as thick as French fries. Place in 8x12-inch baking dish. Cover potatoes with sugar and salt. Sprinkle cinnamon or nutmeg over sugar; more can be used, if desired. Cover with pieces of butter. Twist slices of lemon over this and place lemon peel in with potatoes. Sift flour evenly over potatoes. Add water to mixture so it may be barely seen. Bake at 400° for 1 hour, or until potatoes are done and sugar and butter make a thick syrup. Baste potatoes frequently with syrup. Serves 4–6.

(Country Favorites)

Blushing Apples

Nice meat accompaniment.

2 cups sugar
2 tablespoons red hot candies
¾ cup water
6 tart apples, peeled, cored, sliced

In large saucepan, dissolve sugar and red hots in water; bring to a boil. Simmer apples in mixture until apples are cooked, turning so all slices are cooked. Serves 6–8.

(Country Favorites)

Pasta, Rice, Etc.

1930
Single Handset
Oval-Base

Although the single handset containing both the receiver and transmitter was developed for operators and repairmen by 1878, it wasn't until 1927 that the single handset telephone was introduced to the general public. The 1927 model had a round base. In 1930 it was redesigned with an elongated base made to compliment the long handset. The dial was also recessed into the front of the phone. Like the Candlestick, only the switchhook and switch were contained in the phone. The network and ringer were contained in a subset that was mounted on the wall. The subsets contained a new induction coil that would be used for nearly twenty years.

Greek-Style Macaroni Bake

¾–1 pound ground beef
½ cup chopped onion
1 (6-ounce) can tomato paste
¼ teaspoon ground cinnamon (optional)
½ cup salad dressing or mayonnaise
½ cup all-purpose flour
2 cups milk
2 eggs
⅓ cup grated Parmesan cheese
¼ teaspoon ground nutmeg (optional)
8 ounces elbow macaroni, cooked, drained

Brown beef and onion; drain. Stir in tomato paste, cinnamon, and salad dressing. Combine flour and milk; gradually stir into mixture. Cook and stir over medium heat until thick (do not boil). Beat eggs, cheese, and nutmeg together; gradually stir into sauce. Spoon ½ of macaroni into 2-quart oblong baking dish. Cover with ½ meat sauce. Layer remaining ingredients; bake at 350° for 45 minutes, or until set. Serves 4.

Lou Ann Chism (Cookins for Gulf Coast Council / Blue)

Creamy Beef and Macaroni

1 pound ground beef
1 (7-ounce) package elbow macaroni, cooked, drained
1 (30-ounce) jar spaghetti sauce
½ cup Miracle Whip dressing
1 cup shredded Cheddar cheese

Brown meat; drain. Stir in macaroni, spaghetti sauce, and Miracle Whip; heat thoroughly. Sprinkle with cheese. Makes 4–6 servings.

(Country Favorites)

Macaroni and Ground Beef

1 pound ground beef
½ small onion, chopped
1 package chili seasoning mix
2 (8-ounce) cans tomato sauce
2 cans water
Salt and pepper to taste
1 (6-ounce) box elbow macaroni
1 (16-slice) package American cheese
Garlic powder (optional)

Brown ground beef; drain. Mix onion, chili mix, tomato sauce, and water; add to ground beef with salt and pepper to taste. Cook on low to medium heat for 30 minutes. Boil macaroni in separate pot 10 minutes; remove from heat, and let stand in hot water till ground beef mixture is done. Drain and rinse macaroni. Put a layer of macaroni in greased 9x13-inch casserole dish. Layer beef mixture, then cheese slices. Sprinkle with garlic powder, if desired. Do this till all ingredients are used, ending with cheese slices. Bake at 350° till evenly melted.

Shirley J. Degas (Our Favorite Recipes)

Texas Matador

1 (10-ounce) package egg noodles
2 pounds ground beef
3 teaspoons salt
½ teaspoon pepper
3 teaspoons sugar
1 (16-ounce) can tomatoes
2 (8-ounce) cans tomato sauce
Garlic powder to taste
1 cup sour cream
1 (3-ounce) package cream cheese, softened
1 cup grated cheese

Cook noodles according to package directions; drain. Brown ground beef with salt, pepper, and sugar in skillet; drain. Add tomatoes, tomato sauce, and garlic powder; cook 10 minutes over low heat. Add noodles, sour cream, and cream cheese. Pour into casserole dish, and bake 35 minutes at 350°. Sprinkle with grated cheese last 5 minutes of baking time. Serves 8.

(Country Favorites)

Easy Asian Chicken and Noodles

1 (8-ounce) skinless chicken breast, halved
1 teaspoon dark sesame oil, divided
1 cup sliced green onions, cut in 1-inch pieces
2 packages cabbage and carrot coleslaw
2 (2.8-ounce) packages chicken-flavor ramen noodles
1½ cups water
1 tablespoon low-salt soy sauce

Cut chicken into small, thin slices. Heat ½ teaspoon oil in large nonstick skillet over medium-high heat. Add chicken and green onions; stir-fry 1 minute. Remove mixture from skillet; keep warm. Heat remaining ½ teaspoon oil in skillet over medium-high heat. Add slaw; stir-fry 1–2 minutes. Remove from skillet; keep warm. Discard 1 seasoning packet from noodle packages. Add water and remaining seasoning packet to skillet; bring to a boil. Break noodles in half; add to water mixture. Cook noodles 2 minutes, or until most of liquid is absorbed, stirring frequently. Stir in chicken mixture, slaw, and soy sauce; cook until thoroughly heated. Season with additional soy sauce, if desired. Makes 4–6 servings.

Frances Shisk (Our Favorite Recipes)

The very first American 911 call was placed on February 16, 1968, in Haleyville, Alabama. Alabama Speaker of the House, Rankin Fite, made the first call from another city hall room. It was answered by Congressman Tom Bevill on a bright red telephone located in the police department. Bob Gallagher, president of the Alabama Telephone Company initiated and directed the overall 911 effort. Bob Fitzgerald, plant manager, designed and engineered the needed circuitry for the first U.S. 911 system.

Low-Fat MexItalian Lasagna

1 (15-ounce) can 97% fat-free turkey chili
1 (16-ounce) can Mexican salsa, drained
1 (4-ounce) can sliced mushrooms, drained (optional)
1 (2½-ounce) can diced black olives (optional)
½ cup diced onion
¼ cup grated Parmesan cheese
1½ teaspoons Italian seasoning
1½ cups fat-free cottage cheese
2½ teaspoons dried parsley flakes
9 lasagna noodles, cooked
1½ cups shredded fat-free mozzarella cheese

Heat oven to 350°. In large bowl, combine chili, salsa, mushrooms, black olives, diced onion, Parmesan cheese, and Italian seasoning. In small bowl, stir together cottage cheese and parsley flakes. Layer noodles, cottage cheese, chili mixture, and mozzarella cheese in a 9x9-inch baking dish coated with vegetable cooking spray. Repeat to make 3 layers. Bake 25–30 minutes, or until lasagna is thoroughly heated. Let stand 10 minutes before serving. Serves 6–9.

(Country Favorites)

Marvelous Manicotti

1 package manicotti noodles
1 pound ground beef
1 teaspoon oregano
1 teaspoon basil
½ teaspoon salt
½ teaspoon pepper
1 (16-ounce) carton ricotta cheese
1 pound shredded mozzarella cheese, divided
2 tablespoons grated Parmesan cheese
1 tablespoon parsley flakes
1 egg, beaten
1 (28-ounce) jar spaghetti sauce, divided

Cook noodles according to package; drain; cool. Brown ground beef; add oregano, basil, salt, and pepper; drain; set aside.

In large bowl, mix ricotta cheese, ¾ of mozzarella cheese, Parmesan cheese, parsley flakes, and egg until well blended. Add meat to mixture and stir well. Grease or spray large baking dish with nonstick spray. Pour layer of spaghetti sauce on bottom. Stuff noodles with mixture and line up in dish. Cover with remaining spaghetti sauce and cheese. Cover tightly with foil and bake at 350° for 30 minutes, or until done. Serves 6–8.

Cathi and Robert Garza (Recipes to Remember)

Creamy Fettucini

6 ounces fettucini
¼ cup butter
2 tablespoons all-purpose flour
½ cup water
½ cup half-and-half
½ cup grated fresh Parmesan
2 teaspoons dried parsley flakes
½ teaspoon black pepper
½ teaspoon garlic powder
½ teaspoon poppy seeds
¼ teaspoon salt

Cook noodles according to package directions, omitting salt; drain and cover. Melt butter in heavy saucepan; add flour, stirring until smooth. Cook 1 minute, stirring constantly. Gradually add water and half-and-half. Stir over heat until thickened. Stir in Parmesan cheese and remaining ingredients. Toss with noodles and serve immediately. Serves 6.

Renate Corner (Our Favorite Recipes)

Spaghetti Casserole

1 box Kraft Tangy Italian Spaghetti (green box), reserve spice pack and Parmesan
1 (8-ounce) carton sour cream
1 (8-ounce) package shredded mozzarella cheese
1 pound hamburger meat
1 (20-ounce) can tomato sauce

Cook spaghetti; drain; spread in 9x13-inch pan. Spread with sour cream, then mozzarella cheese. Cook meat in skillet until color disappears. Add tomato sauce plus package of spices from spaghetti box and a small amount of salt. Cook 10–15 minutes. Pour over layered spaghetti. Top with grated Parmesan cheese (from spaghetti box). Bake at 350° for 25–30 minutes. Serves 8–10.

(Country Favorites)

Spaghetti with Chicken Creole

1 (3-pound) chicken, cut up
1 tablespoon oil
2 medium onions, quartered
3 ribs celery, cut in chunks
1 medium green bell pepper, cut in chunks
1 clove garlic
1 (16-ounce) can tomatoes
1 (8-ounce) can tomato sauce
1 teaspoon plus 1 tablespoon, salt, divided
1 teaspoon chili powder
1 bay leaf
1 tablespoon Worcestershire
1 (10-ounce) package frozen cut okra
2 tablespoons all-purpose flour
3 tablespoons cold water
3 quarts boiling water
1 (8-ounce) package spaghetti

In slow-cooking pot with browning unit (or skillet), brown chicken in oil on all sides; drain, if necessary. Finely chop onions, celery, green pepper, and garlic in food processor. Add to pot with tomatoes, tomato sauce, 1 teaspoon salt, chili powder, bay leaf, Worcestershire, and okra. Cover and cook on low about 4 hours (or 30 minutes in skillet). Mix together flour and cold water until smooth; stir into tomato mixture; cover and cook on high setting 30 minutes (or in skillet till thickened).

In saucepan with boiling water, gradually add spaghetti and 1 tablespoon salt, so that water continues to boil. Cook, uncovered, stirring occasionally, until tender; drain. Serve chicken with spaghetti. Makes 4 servings.

Ora Nell Weber (Cookins for Gulf Coast Council / Red)

Chicken Spaghetti

- **1 large fryer, or 2–3 pounds chicken**
- **2 tablespoons oil**
- **1 large onion, chopped**
- **1 cup chopped celery**
- **2–3 cloves garlic, minced**
- **1 cup chopped green bell pepper**
- **1½ teaspoons paprika**
- **2 (10¾-ounce) cans cream of mushroom soup**
- **1 (4-ounce) can chopped pimentos**
- **1 (8-ounce) package spaghetti**
- **1 (4-ounce) can chopped ripe olives**
- **1 (8-ounce) package sharp Cheddar or Colby Jack cheese**

Boil chicken until tender; debone; reserve broth. Heat oil; sauté onion, celery, garlic, green pepper, and paprika until brown. Add soup, about a quart of broth, pimentos, and boned chicken. Boil spaghetti in remaining broth; drain. Combine with sauce pimentos and olives. Pour into casserole and top with cheese of your choice. Bake 30 minutes at 350°. This makes 2 big casseroles; freeze one prior to baking for later use.

Louise Kosub (Our Favorite Recipes)

Chicken Spaghetti

2 pounds chicken pieces
1 (10¾-ounce) can cream of mushroom soup
1 (10¾-ounce) can cream of chicken soup
1 (1-pound) box Velveeta cheese, chopped
1 (4-ounce) can chopped black olives
Chopped green onions (optional)
Chopped pimentos (optional)
1 (4-ounce) can mushrooms, drained (optional)
1 (7-ounce) package spaghetti

Boil chicken; debone and shred. In medium saucepan, combine soups, cheese, olives, onions, pimentos, mushrooms, and chicken. Bring to a low boil; it will look like a thick creamy sauce. Cook spaghetti in boiling water; drain; mix with creamy sauce. Serves 6–8.

Roxanne Soliz (Recipes to Remember)

Ham Jambalaya

1 pound sliced ham, cut in ½-inch cubes
1 tablespoon butter
1 medium onion, chopped
1 medium green bell pepper, chopped
1 clove garlic, minced
1 (20-ounce) can tomatoes
⅛ teaspoon Tabasco
1 cup meat stock or bouillon
1 cup rice
Chopped parsley

In heavy pan, brown ham lightly in butter. Add onion, green pepper, and garlic; cook 5 minutes. Blend in tomatoes, Tabasco, stock, and rice. Cover tightly; simmer 30 minutes, or until rice is done. Lift with fork occasionally (do not stir). Serve garnished with parsley, if desired. Makes 6 servings.

(Country Favorites)

Jambalaya

1 stick margarine
1 cup chopped onion
½ cup chopped celery
½ cup chopped green bell pepper
4 cloves garlic, minced
2 tablespoons tomato paste
2 cups water, divided
Creole seasoning to taste
1 teaspoon sugar
½ teaspoon cornstarch
4 cups cooked rice
½ cup chopped green onions and parsley

Melt margarine; add onion, celery, bell pepper, and garlic in heavy pot; cook uncovered over medium heat until onions are wilted. Add tomato paste and cook, stirring constantly, about 15 minutes. Add 1½ cups water; season to taste. Add sugar and cook uncovered over medium heat for 40 minutes, stirring occasionally.

Dissolve cornstarch in remaining ½ cup water and add; cook another 5 minutes. Mix ingredients with cooked rice; add green onion tops and parsley; mix again. Serves 8 generous portions as a side dish.

Clayton Weeks (Cookins for Gulf Coast Council / Blue)

Pepper Steak with Rice

A good way to serve rice, and an even better way to save money.

1 pound lean beef round steak, cut ½ inch thick
1 tablespoon paprika
2 tablespoons butter
2 cloves garlic, crushed
1½ cups beef broth
1 cup sliced green onions, including tops
2 green bell peppers, cut in strips
2 tablespoons cornstarch
¼ cup water
¼ cup soy sauce
2 large fresh tomatoes, cut in eighths
3 cups hot cooked rice

Pound steak to ¼-inch thickness, and cut into ¼-inch wide strips. Sprinkle meat with paprika and allow to stand while preparing other ingredients. Using a large skillet, brown meat in butter; add garlic and broth; cover and simmer 30 minutes. Stir in onions and green peppers; cover and cook 5 minutes. Blend cornstarch, water, and soy sauce; stir into meat mixture. Cook, stirring, until clear and thickened, about 3 minutes. Add tomatoes and stir gently. Serve over bed of fluffy rice. Serves 6.

Ora Nell Weber (Cookins for Gulf Coast Council / Blue)

Spanish Rice with Steak

Oil
1 cup long-grain rice
1 large onion, chopped
1 round steak, cut in ½-inch cubes
1 (14½-ounce) can whole tomatoes
1 can water
1 green bell pepper, chopped
Salt and pepper to taste

Put enough oil in heavy skillet to cover bottom. Brown rice and onion together; stir frequently to brown rice evenly and keep from sticking. In another skillet, brown steak in small amount of oil until all red disappears. When rice has browned, add all remaining ingredients to rice in lightly greased casserole, including meat and drippings. Stir together to mix, but don't stir again. Bake, covered at 350° for 20–25 minutes. Serves 4–6.

Tina M. Salinas (Cookins for Gulf Coast Council / Red)

Mexican Rice

2 cups rice
½ cup oil
½ onion, chopped
½ green bell pepper, chopped
1 tablespoon powdered comino (Italian for cumin)
1 garlic clove, chopped
1 (8-ounce) can tomato sauce
8 cups water
Salt to taste

Brown rice in pan with oil. Before all rice is browned, add onion and bell pepper and continue to stir, then add comino, garlic, tomato sauce, and water. Add salt to taste. Bring to a boil, then place on lowest heat and cook 25 minutes. Cover; do not stir anymore. If more water is needed, pour in middle of rice and turn off heat; set aside for a few minutes, covered. Serves 6–8.

Margie Ortiz (Recipes to Remember)

Rice Vera Cruz

- 1 pound lean ground beef, crumbled
- 2 medium onions, chopped
- 1 green bell pepper, chopped
- 2 tablespoons oil or bacon drippings
- 1 (16-ounce) can tomatoes
- 1 (10-ounce) can beef consommé
- ⅓ cup sherry
- 2 teaspoons chili powder
- Salt to taste
- 1 cup sliced ripe olives
- 1 cup rice
- 1 cup grated Cheddar cheese

Cook beef, onions, and green pepper in oil until brown, stirring frequently; drain. Add tomatoes, consommé, sherry, chili powder, salt, and olives; bring to a boil. Stir in rice slowly and cook several minutes. Pour into a 2-quart casserole and cover. Bake at 375° for 30 minutes. Uncover; stir with a fork. Sprinkle cheese over top and bake 15 minutes longer. Let stand 5–10 minutes before serving. Makes 6 servings.

Donna Wilcox (Cookins for Gulf Coast Council / Red)

Barbecued Rice

- 1⅓ cups instant rice
- ⅔ cup hot ketchup
- ⅔ cup water
- ¼ cup chopped onion
- 2 tablespoons chopped green bell pepper
- ½ teaspoon salt
- 2 tablespoons margarine

Form a pouch with heavy-duty foil. Put all ingredients except margarine in foil; mix well, being careful not to tear foil. Dot with margarine and seal pouch tightly. Place on grill (or in oven) and cook over moderate heat approximately 30 minutes. Serves 4.

Alieen Julian (Cookins for Gulf Coast Council / Red)

Sausage Rice Stuffing Casserole

1 pound pork sausage
2 cups chopped celery
2 cups chopped onions
2 cups sliced fresh mushrooms or (16-ounce) can, drained
1 cup chicken broth
4 cups cooked brown rice
2 teaspoons salt
½ teaspoon pepper
⅓ teaspoon crushed dried sage
1 teaspoon poultry seasoning
½ cup slivered almonds

Cook sausage, celery, onions, and mushrooms in large skillet until meat is browned; drain. Combine with remaining ingredients and place in greased 3-quart casserole. Cover and bake at 350° for 45 minutes. Yields 8–10 servings.

Note: May be used to stuff a large turkey.

(Country Favorites)

Herbed Rice Pilaf

2 cups uncooked long-grain rice
1 cup chopped celery
½ cup chopped onion
¼ cup butter
4 cups chicken broth
1 teaspoon Worcestershire
1 teaspoon soy sauce
1 teaspoon dried oregano
1 teaspoon dried thyme

In skillet, sauté rice, celery, and onion in butter until rice is lightly browned and vegetables are tender. Spoon into greased 2-quart casserole. Combine all remaining ingredients; pour over rice mixture. Cover and bake at 325° for 50 minutes, or until rice is done. Serves 8.

(Country Favorites)

Dirty Rice

1 pound country sausage, hot or sage
½ link Italian sausage
¼ cup chopped celery
½ cup chopped onion
1 (4-ounce) can mushroom bits and pieces, drained
1 (8-ounce) can LeSueur peas, drained
Salt and pepper to taste
2 cups cooked rice

Cook sausages and drain; remove from skillet. Sauté celery and onion in sausage drippings. Combine all ingredients and heat thoroughly. Serves 6.

Claudie Schmidt (Cookins for Gulf Coast Council / Red)

Quick Dirty Rice

1 box Uncle Ben's instant brown rice
2 (10¾-ounce) cans cream of mushroom soup
1 (1-pound) package sausage, browned, drained

Mix all together. Bake in greased casserole dish at 350° until edges brown, about 25 minutes.

Betty Hatcher (Our Favorite Recipes)

Buttered Rice

2 tablespoons butter
2 medium onions, diced
2 cups rice
2 cups hot consommé
2 teaspoons salt
1 tablespoon chopped parsley

Melt butter in covered pot and sauté onions. Add rice; stir until grains are well coated with butter. Add consommé and salt; stir and cover. Simmer over low heat about 30 minutes, until grains are tender and liquid absorbed. Toss rice lightly with fork to release steam and put over warm burner without lid until each grain is separated. Toss rice with butter and chopped parsley before serving. Excellent with wild game. Serves 8.

(Country Favorites)

Herbed Orange Rice

⅔ cup chopped celery with leaves
2 tablespoons minced onion
¼ cup butter or margarine
1½ cups water
1 cup orange juice
1 tablespoon grated orange peel
1 teaspoon salt
⅛ teaspoon crushed thyme leaves
1 cup long-grain rice

In 2-quart saucepan over medium heat, cook celery and onion in hot butter till tender, about 5 minutes. Add water, orange juice, orange peel, salt, and thyme. Heat to boiling; stir in rice; reduce to low heat, cover, and simmer 15–20 minutes, until rice is tender and all liquid is absorbed. Fluff with fork and serve. Serves 4–6.

David Cleland (Recipes to Remember)

Pork-Rice Tamale Pie

1 cup uncooked rice
1 (8-ounce) can tomatoes or tomato purée
½ cup sliced green olives
3–4 ripe olives, sliced (optional)
2 teaspoons chili powder
2 cups finely chopped, cooked pork
1 cup meat broth
Biscuit dough

Wash rice through several waters until water is clear; drain. Add gradually to a large quantity of rapidly boiling salted water, never allowing water to stop boiling during the addition. Boil rapidly, uncovered, until rice is tender, 15–20 minutes, then drain. Combine rice, tomatoes, olives, seasoning, cooked pork, and meat broth. Pour into well-greased casserole or baking dish and bake in moderate 350° oven 30 minutes. Cut small biscuits from biscuit dough, and place on top of pork-rice casserole; return to oven and bake at 400° until biscuits are done. Serve while hot.

Note: If broth is not available, substitute 1 beef bouillon cube dissolved in 1 cup boiling water.

(Country Favorites)

Wild Rice

2 bunches green onions, chopped
2 cups chopped celery
1 green bell pepper, chopped
1 (8-ounce) can sliced mushrooms, drained
2 tablespoons butter
1 package hot sausage
1 package mild sausage
1 cup white rice
1 package wild and long-grain rice
1 package wild and brown rice

Sauté onions, celery, pepper, and mushrooms in butter. Cook sausage, drain, and add to mixture. Cook all rice according to package directions. Mix all ingredients; place in greased large baking pan; bake for 1 hour at 350°. This is good with turkey and cranberry sauce. Serves 8–10.

Audrey Morgan (Cookins for Gulf Coast Council / Red)

Cornbread and Sausage Quiche

6 large eggs, beaten
¾ cup milk
1½ cups grated Cheddar or Monterey Jack cheese
1 (4-ounce) can diced green chiles
2 (8-ounce) packages brown 'n serve sausages, crumbled
1 (6-ounce) bag cornbread stuffing
Salsa and sour cream (optional)

Preheat oven to 425°. Whisk together eggs and milk. Add cheese, chiles, and sausage; blend well. Fold in stuffing; mix well. Pour mixture into 7x11-inch baking dish sprayed with cooking spray; cover and bake 40 minutes, or until eggs are set. Top with salsa and sour cream, if desired. Serves 6.

GeraLyn "Gerri" Gray (Our Favorite Recipes)

Mexican Quiche

5 ounces diced Monterey Jack cheese
3 ounces diced Cheddar cheese
1 jalapeño pepper, seeded, sliced
1 green bell pepper, diced
1 (9-inch) pie shell, unbaked
¼ stick butter
½ large onion, sliced
½ pound ground beef
1 teaspoon chili powder
1 teaspoon tomato paste

Sprinkle cheeses and peppers in bottom of pie shell. Melt butter in heavy skillet; add onion, meat, and chili powder; sauté until light brown. Combine with tomato paste; cover peppers and cheeses in pie shell. Pour Quiche Custard Mix over and bake 20 minutes at 400°, then 20 minutes at 325°.

QUICHE CUSTARD MIX:

4 eggs
1½ cups light cream or milk
¼ teaspoon nutmeg
¼ teaspoon salt
Dash of pepper
2 drops Tabasco
½ cup freshly grated Parmesan cheese
1 teaspoon chopped fresh parsley

Use a wire whisk or electric beater to beat ingredients, except cheese and parsley, in a large bowl. Stir in Parmesan and parsley. May be used for any quiche.

Bert Atwood (Cookins for Gulf Coast Council / Blue)

Hashbrown Quiche

3 cups frozen loose-pack shredded hashbrowns, thawed
½ cup butter, melted
1 cup diced fully cooked ham
1 cup shredded Cheddar cheese
¼ cup diced green bell pepper
2 eggs
½ cup milk
½ teaspoon salt
¼ teaspoon pepper

Blot hashbrowns between paper towels to remove excess moisture. Press into bottom and up sides of ungreased 9-inch pie plate. Drizzle with butter; bake at 425° for 25 minutes. Combine ham, cheese, and green pepper; spoon over crust. In a small bowl, beat eggs, milk, salt, and pepper; pour over all. Reduce heat to 350° and bake 25–30 minutes, or until a knife inserted near center comes out clean. Allow to stand 10 minutes before cutting. Serves 6.

(Country Favorites)

Chili Cheese Strata

- 1 (12-ounce) loaf French bread, cut in 1-inch cubes
- 2 cups shredded Cheddar or Monterey Jack cheese, divided
- 1 (8-ounce) jar mild green chile salsa, or 1 (4-ounce) can chopped green chiles and 4-ounce jar salsa, combined
- 4 eggs
- 2 cups milk or half-and-half
- 2 tablespoons minced onion
- 1 tablespoon Worcestershire
- 1 (10¾-ounce) can Cheddar cheese soup, undiluted
- Paprika

In greased 2-quart casserole, arrange bread cubes evenly. Sprinkle 1 cup cheese over cubes. Pour chile salsa over to cover evenly; set aside. In large bowl, mix together next 5 ingredients; pour over bread. Top with remaining cheese. Cover; refrigerate 6 hours or overnight.

Uncover; dust with paprika. Bake at 350° for 30 minutes, or until lightly browned and bubbly. Yields 8 servings.

(Country Favorites)

Meats

1937
"300" Series

An innovation in telephone design was the placing of the bell in the base of the "300" Series desk set. The "300" Series was the first model that included the ringer, coil, and capacitor in the base, forming a complete phone in one package. Previous models required an external subset that contained these components. The "300" Series was made from 1936 until 1954. Earlier versions had housings made of die-cast metal but thermo-plastic was substituted in the early 1940s due to the onset of World War II.

Soon crossbar switching was introduced, and automation came to long-distance switching. Dialed routing codes soon gave way to the familiar area codes, which the switch itself could translate into the needed routing information. Call completion time dropped to 10–20 seconds.

Hamburger Steaks with Sautéed Mushrooms and Onions

1 package sliced fresh mushrooms
1½ cups red wine (Merlot or Cabernet Sauvignon)
1 white onion, peeled, sliced
1 envelope brown gravy mix (optional)
1 pound ground beef
1 envelope onion soup mix

Place mushrooms in bowl with red wine, making sure to gently mix so that all mushrooms are marinated; set aside. Add sliced onion to bowl; set aside. If using gravy mix, prepare as directed on package. Place ground beef and onion soup mix in bowl. Shape mixture into patties, about 1 inch thick. Place in skillet over medium heat. Make sure not to flip patties until a darker outer crust has formed (since you only flip once). At the same time the patties are cooking, place a small pat of butter in a separate skillet and sauté the onion until golden brown; remove from skillet; sauté mushrooms. As they reduce, there will be a considerable amount of liquid in the bottom of the pan. Pour it off and set aside (do not discard). Continue cooking mushrooms until brown; combine with onion.

Once patties are almost ready, pour liquid wine reduction (salvaged from mushrooms) over patties. Cover patties with mushrooms and onion. (If using gravy mix, heat gravy in skillet and stir in wine reduction and pour over patties, then top with mushrooms and onions.) Turn off heat and let simmer until mushrooms and onions are warm; serve. Serves 4.

Jeannie Higgins (Our Favorite Recipes)

Oven Porcupines

1 pound hamburger meat
½ cup uncooked rice
1½ cups water, divided
1 teaspoon salt
½ teaspoon celery salt
⅛ teaspoon garlic salt
⅛ teaspoon pepper
1 (8-ounce) can tomato sauce
⅓ cup chopped onion
2 tablespoons Worcestershire

Heat oven to 350°. Mix meat, rice, ½ cup water, salts, and pepper. Shape mixture by rounded tablespoonfuls into balls. Place meatballs in ungreased 8x8-inch baking dish. Stir together remaining ingredients; pour over meatballs. Cover with aluminum foil. Bake 45 minutes; uncover and bake 15 minutes more. Makes 4–6 servings.

(Country Favorites)

Most adults remember when AT&T split off its "Baby Bell" companies in 1982. But did you know that one of those "Babies" actually bought out "Ma Bell" herself? In 2005, SBC Communications—one of the divested Regional Bell Operating Companies—acquired the original AT&T Corp. and changed its name to AT&T Inc.

Hamburger-Corn Casserole

1½ pounds lean ground beef
1 cup chopped onion
1 (15-ounce) can whole-kernel corn, drained
1 (10¾-ounce) can cream of chicken soup
1 (10¾-ounce) can cream of mushroom soup
1 cup sour cream
¼ cup chopped pimento
¾ teaspoon salt
¼ teaspoon pepper
1 (5-ounce) package noodles, cooked, drained
1 cup soft bread crumbs
3 tablespoons butter, melted

Lightly brown beef in heavy skillet or Dutch oven; add chopped onion and cook until tender, but not browned. Add corn, soups, sour cream, pimento, salt, and pepper. Stir in cooked noodles, drained; spoon mixture into a 4-quart casserole dish. Mix bread crumbs with melted butter and sprinkle over top. Bake at 350° for 30 minutes. Serves 8–10.

Esther Hays (Cookins for Gulf Coast Council)

Beef Salami

2 pounds ground meat (or half venison, half beef)
1 cup water
2 tablespoons salt
1½ tablespoons liquid smoke
¼ teaspoon garlic powder
½ teaspoon onion powder
1 teaspoon mustard seeds
1 teaspoon cracked black pepper

Combine all ingredients and mix thoroughly by hand. Shape in 3 (6-inch) rolls. Wrap each in plastic wrap. Fasten end securely. Refrigerate 24 hours.

Remove plastic; place on rack with drip pan. Bake at 300° for 1½ hours.

Louise Kosub (Our Favorite Recipes)

Western Beef and Corn Pie

CRUST:

1 cup all-purpose flour
½ cup yellow cornmeal
2 tablespoons sugar
1 teaspoon baking powder
1 teaspoon salt
½ cup milk
¼ cup butter, softened
1 egg
1 cup shredded Cheddar cheese, divided

Combine all ingredients, except ½ cup cheese, in large bowl; mix well. Spread over bottom and sides of greased 9-inch deep dish pie pan.

FILLING:

1 pound ground chuck
½ teaspoon salt
½ teaspoon chili powder
1 (12-ounce) can Mexicorn
1 (6-ounce) can tomato paste
⅔ cup barbecue sauce
1 cup shredded Cheddar cheese

Heat oven to 400°. In large frypan, brown ground chuck; drain. Stir in remaining Filling ingredients; mix well. Pour Filling into Crust; sprinkle with remaining ½ cup cheese. Bake at 400° for 25–30 minutes.

Donna Wilcox (Cookins for Gulf Coast Council / Red)

Beefed-Up Biscuit Casserole

1½ pounds ground chuck
½ cup chopped onion
¼ cup chopped green bell pepper
1 (8-ounce) can tomato sauce
2 teaspoons chili powder
¾ teaspoon garlic powder
1 (10-count) can flaky biscuits, divided
1½ cups grated cheese, divided
½ cup sour cream
1 egg, beaten

Brown meat, onion, and bell pepper in large skillet; drain well. Stir in tomato sauce, chili powder, and garlic powder. Simmer while preparing dough.

Separate 5 biscuits making 10; press into greased 9x9-inch baking dish. Combine ½ cup cheese, sour cream, and egg in bowl; mix well. Remove meat from heat; stir in cheese mixture; pour over dough. Separate remaining 5 biscuits making 10; cover meat mixture. Sprinkle rest of cheese over top of biscuits. Bake at 350° for 25–30 minutes.

(Country Favorites)

Cut 'n' Shoot Casserole

½ stick butter
3 medium onions, chopped
2 cloves garlic, chopped
2–4 pounds sirloin, cut into strips
Flour
3 (10¾-ounce) cans cream of chicken soup
1 (10¾-ounce) can cream of celery soup
2 (10-ounce) cans Ro-Tel tomatoes
12–14 corn tortillas
1 cup grated American cheese, divided

Spray 11x22-inch casserole dish with cooking spray. Melt butter in pan; add onions, garlic, and sirloin strips; sauté. Add enough flour to thicken juice. Warm soups and tomatoes in saucepan. Warm tortillas in hot oil, then blot excess oil with paper towels. Make 2 layers in pan with tortillas, soup mixture, meat mixture, then top with cheese, reserving ¼ cup cheese. Cover dish with foil and bake in 350° oven until bubbly. Top with remaining cheese and allow it to melt. Especially good when made the day before.

Linda O'Dell (Our Favorite Recipes)

Emma M. Nutt was the first female employee for the Bell Telephone Company. She was hired at the Boston exchange September 1, 1878, and continued until her retirement in 1915. Her 37 years as an operator began a tradition of long service.

Ranch Hand Mexican Pie

Enough prepared mashed potatoes for 4 servings
1 egg, slightly beaten
¼ cup sliced green onions with tops
1 pound ground beef
½ cup chopped onion
1 (8-ounce) can tomato sauce
¼ cup sliced ripe olives
2–3 teaspoons chili powder
¼ teaspoon salt
¼ teaspoon garlic powder
1 cup shredded Cheddar or Monterey Jack cheese
Sour cream, chopped bell pepper, tomato, and avocado for garnish (optional)

Heat oven to 425°. Grease 9-inch pie plate. Place mashed potatoes in bowl; stir in egg and green onions. Spread and press potato mixture evenly against bottom and side of pie plate. Bake 20–25 minutes, or until light brown. Cook ground beef and chopped onion in 10-inch skillet, stirring occasionally, until beef is brown; drain. Stir in remaining ingredients except cheese. Cover and cook over low heat 5 minutes, stirring occasionally. Spoon into shell; sprinkle with cheese. Bake 2–3 minutes, or until cheese is melted. If desired, garnish with sour cream, green bell pepper, tomato, and avocado. Serves 6.

Ofe Gonzales (Recipes to Remember)

Hamburger Potato Pie

1 medium onion, chopped
2 tablespoons butter
1 pound ground beef
½ teaspoon salt
½ teaspoon pepper
1 cup cooked peas
2 cups diced tomatoes
½ cup ketchup
5 potatoes, cooked, mashed
1 egg

Brown onion in butter. Remove onion, and brown ground beef with salt and pepper. Combine and place ground beef and onion, peas, tomatoes, and ketchup in a casserole dish. Beat mashed potatoes with egg and spoon on top of meat mixture. Brown in 375° oven until peaks are golden.

(Country Favorites)

Poppin' Fresh Barbecups

Great for something in a hurry—these barbecups will be "poppin'" from your oven in just minutes.

¾ pound ground beef
½ cup barbecue sauce
1 tablespoon instant minced onion, or ¼ cup chopped onion
2 tablespoons firmly packed brown sugar
1 (10-ounce) can Hungry Jack refrigerated big flaky biscuits
1 cup shredded Cheddar or American cheese

Heat oven to 400°. Grease 10 muffin cups. Brown ground beef; drain. Add barbecue sauce, onion, and brown sugar. Separate biscuit dough into 10 biscuits. Place each biscuit in greased muffin cup, pressing dough to cover bottom and sides. Spoon meat mixture into each cup. Sprinkle each with cheese; bake at 400° for 10–12 minutes or until golden brown. Loosen with spatula and remove from pans. Serve immediately.

Donna Wilcox (Cookins for Gulf Coast Council / Blue).

Firecracker Enchilada Casserole

2 pounds ground beef
1 large onion, chopped
2 tablespoons chili powder
2–3 teaspoons ground cumin
1 teaspoon salt
1 (15-ounce) can ranch-style beans
6 corn tortillas
1½ cups shredded Monterey Jack cheese
1½ cups shredded Cheddar cheese
1 (10-ounce) can Ro-Tel tomatoes
1 (10¾-ounce) can cream of mushroom soup

Cook beef and onion in large skillet until meat is brown and onion is tender; discard pan drippings. Add chili powder, cumin, and salt; stir well. Place meat mixture in 9x13-inch baking pan. Layer beans, tortillas, and cheese over meat mixture. Pour Ro-Tel over cheese. Spread soup over all. Cover baking pan; refrigerate overnight.

Bake, uncovered, at 350° for 1 hour. Serves 8–10.

Kay Bauch (Cookins for Gulf Coast Council / Red)

Enchilada Casserole

1 (8-count) package corn tortillas
1½ pounds lean ground beef
½ onion, chopped
1 (15-ounce) can ranch-style beans
1 (10-ounce) can diced tomatoes and green chiles
1 (10¾-ounce) can cream of chicken soup
2 cups grated Cheddar cheese, divided

Quarter tortillas; layer half in bottom of 9x13-inch pan. Brown ground meat with onion; drain. Add beans, tomatoes and green chiles, and soup. Simmer 15 minutes. Pour half of mixture on top of tortillas. Top with half of cheese. Repeat layers. Bake in preheated 350° oven 30 minutes. Serves 6–8.

Karen Strickland (Recipes to Remember)

Flautas

2 pounds ground beef
3 tablespoons chili powder
Salt and pepper to taste
1 tablespoon ground cumin
2 tablespoons flour
Water
Lettuce, chopped
Tomatoes, chopped
Grated Cheddar cheese
20 small tortillas
Guacamole
Sour cream

Sauté ground beef until all pink has disappeared. Add chili powder, salt and pepper, and cumin. Sprinkle flour over meat. When flour is absorbed, add enough water to moisten. Place meat mixture, lettuce, tomatoes, and cheese in hot tortillas; fold tortillas and top with guacamole and dabs of sour cream. Serve at once. Serves 10.

Donna Wilcox (Cookins for Gulf Coast Council / Red)

Hot Tamale Pie

1 large onion
1 large green bell pepper
1 small stalk celery
1–2 teaspoons oil
2 pounds lean ground beef, browned
1 teaspoon salt
1 package chili mix
1 (8-ounce) can tomato sauce
1 package cornbread mix
1 cup evaporated milk
1 (8-ounce) package shredded Cheddar cheese

Preheat oven to 400°. Sauté onion, green pepper, and celery in a little oil for 10 minutes. Mix with meat in greased 9x13-inch baking dish; add salt, chili mix, and tomato sauce. In separate bowl, mix cornbread mix and milk together; pour over top of meat mixture and sprinkle with cheese. Bake 20–25 minutes. Serves 8–10.

Anita Vela (Our Favorite Recipes)

Mom's Cabbage Rolls

1 large head cabbage
1 pound ground beef
1 pound ground pork
½ pound sausage
1½ cups rice, uncooked
Salt and pepper to taste
4 cloves garlic, minced, divided
2 (28-ounce) jars sauerkraut
1 (29-ounce) can tomato juice
Water

Core cabbage and blanch in large pot of water to soften leaves; separate and drain. Mix beef, pork, sausage, and rice. Add salt, pepper, and 2 cloves minced garlic to meat. Place small ball of meat mixture in center of cabbage leaf. Fold cabbage leaf around and secure with toothpicks. Repeat until all meat is used. Place rolls in a large stockpot. Cover with sauerkraut, tomato juice, and remaining garlic. Add water until cabbage rolls are covered. Simmer on low heat 6–8 hours. Best to refrigerate and reheat next day.

Debra Martin (Our Favorite Recipes)

Margie's Recipe

1 pound ground lean beef
½ cup chopped celery
½ cup chopped onion
½ cup chopped green bell pepper
½ (8-ounce) bag shell macaroni
2 (15-ounce) cans Veg-All vegetables, drained
1 (15-ounce) can sliced white potatoes, drained
1 (8-ounce) can hominy, drained
1 (8-ounce) can sliced mushrooms, drained
½ (4-ounce) jar pimentos, drained
1 (8-ounce) can sliced pitted ripe olives, drained
1 (10¾-ounce) can cream of mushroom soup
1 (8-ounce) can tomato sauce
1 cup each: grated Velveeta and Longhorn Cheddar

Brown meat, remove from grease, and drain on paper towels. To drippings add celery, onion, and bell pepper; sauté till tender. Cook macaroni; drain well. Add canned vegetables and meat to macaroni. Stir in soup and tomato sauce; stir well. Spoon into dish alternating layers of mixture and combined cheeses, ending with cheese. Bake at 400° for 45 minutes.

Margie Case (Cookins for Gulf Coast Council / Red)

Michelle's Meatloaf

2 pounds lean ground beef
¼ cup diced onion
Salt and pepper to taste
1 egg
4–6 thin slices ham
4–6 thin slices cheese
1 (8-ounce) can tomato sauce

Preheat oven to 350°. In large bowl, mix meat, onion, salt, pepper, and egg. On a flat surface, spread meat mixture out in the shape of a rectangle to about 1 inch thick. This can be done in a 9x13-inch dish or on your counter, covered with plastic wrap. Cover meat mixture with ham and cheese slices, leaving a 1-inch border on all sides. Roll mixture up jellyroll-style until mixture resembles a loaf. Seal ends by crimping meat together in baking dish. Cover with entire can of tomato sauce. Cover with foil and bake 1 hour, or until juices run clear. Serves 8–10.

Michelle Stuyvesant (Recipes to Remember)

Marinated Minute Steaks

¾ cup oil
¼ cup soy sauce
3 tablespoons honey
2 tablespoons vinegar
2 teaspoons minced green onions
1½ teaspoons ginger
⅛ teaspoon garlic powder
6 minute or cube steaks

Combine all ingredients except steaks in plastic bag or shallow pan. Add steaks; let stand 1–2 hours. Grill or broil 4–5 inches from hot coals or broiler for 5–7 minutes on each side, brushing frequently with marinade. Serves 6.

Verna Dvorak (Cookins for Gulf Coast Council / Red)

Beef and Spinach Stir-Fry

1 pound boneless top round
2 tablespoons oil
1 cup sliced mushrooms
½ cup chopped green onions
1 cup thinly sliced celery
1 cup hot water
2 tablespoons cornstarch
1 tablespoon sugar
1 tablespoon lemon juice
1 tablespoon soy sauce
1 teaspoon salt
1 teaspoon beef bouillon
½ pound fresh spinach
Cooked rice

Cut beef into thin strips against the grain. Heat oil in wok or heavy skillet. Add beef and stir-fry till browned. Add next 3 ingredients; stir-fry till crisp-tender. Combine water, cornstarch, sugar, lemon juice, soy sauce, salt, and bouillon. Add to beef mixture; cook and stir till mixture thickens. Add spinach to beef mixture, stirring just to coat and warm spinach leaves. Serve over rice. Serves 4.

Hildegarde Brinkmeyer (Cookins for Gulf Coast Council / Red)

Korean Beef

3 pounds boneless roast beef, thinly sliced
3 teaspoons white wine
2½ tablespoons sugar
2 teaspoons MSG
2 teaspoons black pepper
5 large cloves garlic, minced
1 teaspoon powdered ginger
1 bunch green onions with 1½-inch tops, chopped fine
8 tablespoons soy sauce
8 tablespoons water
2 tablespoons sesame oil
Safflower oil for frying

Slice beef slices into matchstick-size pieces. Combine all ingredients and marinate beef 24 hours.

Reserve marinade. Fry beef quickly in hot safflower oil. When all meat is cooked, pour in remaining marinade and simmer a few minutes. Serve with rice. Serves 6–8.

Linda Cline (Cookins for Gulf Coast Council / Red)

Hot Spicy Pepper Steak

3 tablespoons soy sauce
1 teaspoon Worcestershire
¾ teaspoon ginger
1½ tablespoons cornstarch
¾ cup picante sauce
4 tablespoons oil, divided
2 pounds tenderized beef round steak, cut into 1½x¼-inch strips
1 clove garlic, minced
1 medium red or green bell pepper, sliced
1 cup sliced fresh mushrooms
6 green onions, diced
¾ cup water
2 cups cooked rice

Combine soy sauce, Worcestershire, ginger, cornstarch, and picante sauce in small bowl; set aside. Over high heat in large skillet or wok, heat 2 tablespoons oil until hot, but not smoking. Add meat; stir-fry 2–3 minutes; drain; set aside. Heat remaining 2 tablespoons oil in skillet. Add garlic, peppers, mushrooms, and onions; stir-fry 3 minutes. Return meat to skillet; stir in picante sauce mixture; add water; cook and stir about 1 minute or until sauce thickens. Serve over hot rice.

(Country Favorites)

Marinated Brisket

1 tablespoon onion salt
2 teaspoons celery salt
1 (4-ounce) bottle liquid smoke
1 (3- to 4-pound) brisket
2 tablespoons A1 Sauce
4 tablespoons Worcestershire

Rub seasonings on brisket. Make sure to rub both sides. Place brisket in foil-lined pan and pour in sauces. Cover with foil and refrigerate overnight.

Bake in 250° oven 6–7 hours. Place pan of water underneath while cooking. Drippings make good gravy.

(Country Favorites)

Oven BBQ Brisket

3 tablespoons liquid smoke
1 (3- to 4-pound) brisket, boned, trimmed
Celery salt to taste
Onion salt to taste
Garlic salt to taste
Salt and pepper to taste
3 tablespoons Worcestershire
1 (6-ounce) bottle BBQ sauce

Pour liquid smoke over meat. Generously sprinkle both sides with celery, onion, and garlic salts. Cover and refrigerate overnight; do not drain meat.

Sprinkle meat with salt and pepper to taste, and Worcestershire. Bake in 350° oven 5 hours, covered. Pour BBQ sauce over; bake uncovered 1 hour. Serves a lot.

Deedee Mize (Cookins for Gulf Coast Council / Red)

Beef Burgundy

¼ cup all-purpose flour
½ teaspoon salt
¼ teaspoon pepper
2 pounds boneless chuck, cut into 1½-inch cubes
5 tablespoons butter, divided
1 envelope beef-flavor mushroom mix
2 cups water
1 cup burgundy or any dry wine
1 bay leaf
½ teaspoon oregano
½ teaspoon basil
⅛ teaspoon garlic powder
1 tablespoon sugar
½ pound small white onions, peeled
5 medium carrots, pared, cut into 1½-inch pieces

Combine flour, salt, and pepper; dredge beef cubes in mixture. In 4- to 5-quart heavy saucepan, melt 3 tablespoons butter; brown beef well on all sides. Remove from pan. Combine beef-mushroom mix, water, wine, and herbs. Stir into drippings in pan; cook, stirring constantly, until slightly thickened. Return meat to pan; reduce heat and simmer, covered, 2 hours.

In large skillet, melt remaining 2 tablespoons butter; add sugar, then brown onions and carrots, stirring frequently, until nicely glazed. Add vegetables to meat in saucepan and cook an additional 30 minutes, or until vegetables are tender. Serves 6–8.

Ora Nell Weber (Cookins for Gulf Coast Council / Blue)

Village Special Swiss Steak

2 pounds beef round, cut into 4 servings
1 cup all-purpose flour
1 teaspoon paprika
Salt and pepper to taste
3 tablespoons shortening
1 medium onion, chopped
1 (10¾-ounce) can tomato soup
1 teaspoon Ac'cent
1 tablespoon ketchup
1 garlic button, chopped
1 (8-ounce) can mushrooms, diced
1 ounce sherry wine

Press steaks into combined flour and paprika, seasoned with salt and pepper to taste; pound into meat. Braise steaks in melted shortening. When brown on both sides, add remaining ingredients and bake 30 minutes. Serves 4.

Johnnie Johnson (Cookins for Gulf Coast Council / Red)

Short Ribs with Lima Beans

2 cups large dry lima beans
5 cups water
3 pounds short ribs
½ cup ketchup
½ cup chopped onions
½ cup chopped celery
1 clove garlic, minced
3 teaspoons salt, or to taste
Pepper to taste

Rinse limas; add to 5 cups water in large kettle; boil 2 minutes, remove from heat and let stand 1 hour. Brown ribs in skillet; remove excess fat. Bury ribs in limas; add remaining ingredients. Cover and cook gently until meat and limas are tender, 45 minutes to 1 hour. If needed, add more water, and season with more salt and pepper in last ½ hour of cooking.

(Country Favorites)

Hawaiian Pork Chops

6 medium sweet potatoes, peeled, quartered
4 or 5 pork chops
Salt to taste
4 or 5 slices pineapple
¼ cup pineapple juice

Slice potatoes in medium slices; set aside. Heat cast-iron skillet to hot (no grease); put pork chops in and let brown on one side. Lower heat and turn pork chops; add salt. Add sweet potatoes all around skillet. Place pineapple slices on chops; add juice. Cover with tight lid and turn heat to low. Simmer about 45 minutes, or until potatoes are tender. Serves 4–5.

Nancy Blue (Cookins for Gulf Coast Council / Blue)

Oriental Pork Chops

¼ cup soy sauce
¼ cup pineapple juice
⅓ cup oil
1 tablespoon grated orange peel
⅓ cup orange juice
2 tablespoons chopped green bell pepper
¼ cup teriyaki sauce
1 tablespoon ginger
2 tablespoons brown sugar
4–6 pork loin chops, cut 1–1¼ inches thick

In glass dish, combine all ingredients, except pork chops. Add pork chops; cover and marinate 3 or 4 hours in refrigerator.

Place chops on grill 5–7 inches above coals. Cook at low temperature 20–25 minutes, or until done, turning chops occasionally and brushing frequently with marinade. Serves 4–6.

(Country Favorites)

Frankfurters with Hamburger Sauce

3–4 small onions, chopped
1 tablespoon fat
½ pound ground beef
1 teaspoon chili powder
1 teaspoon salt
1 teaspoon sugar
1 (20-ounce) can crushed tomatoes
1 pound frankfurters
Long rolls or buns

Brown onions in fat; add hamburger and cook a few minutes, tossing with fork. Drain. Add remaining ingredients, except frankfurters and buns, and simmer gently 45 minutes. Prepare frankfurters to suit individual taste, either, boil, steam, or broil. Split long rolls, place franks in center and fill center cavity with hamburger sauce. Serve very hot. Serves 6–8.

(Country Favorites)

Hot Dogs with Cheesy Corn Topping

1 (7-ounce) can Niblets corn, drained
1 cup shredded reduced-fat Cheddar cheese
¼ cup reduced-calorie mayonnaise
2 tablespoons chopped green onions (optional)
10 turkey/beef franks
10 hot dog buns

In small bowl, combine corn, cheese, mayonnaise, and green onions; mix well. Place franks in buns; spoon topping over; wrap each bun in heavy-duty foil. Grill 4–6 minutes on medium heat or 10–15 minutes on low heat until thoroughly heated. Or bake in 350° oven 15–20 minutes on cookie sheet, or until cheese is melted.

(Country Favorites)

Stuffed Franks

4 slices bacon
½ cup chopped celery
¼ cup chopped onion
½ cup ketchup
10 frankfurters
½ cup grated American cheese

Fry bacon till crisp; drain, saving 2 tablespoons drippings. Crumble bacon; set aside. Sauté celery and onion in drippings till tender; stir in ketchup. Split franks lengthwise, being careful not to cut all the way through. Fill with mixture; bake at 425° for 15 minutes. Sprinkle with bacon and cheese. Return to oven till cheese is melted; serve hot. Serves 5.

Carol Patterson (Cookins for Gulf Coast Council / Red)

Poultry

1954
"500" Series

With the invention of the transistor in 1947, the vacuum tube transmitter was soon replaced. Equipment size was reduced and reliability increased, making telephone service more affordable. The telephone started to become a decorative household item in the early 1950s. Although some colored telephones were available much earlier, they did not gain widespread popularity until the advent of the "500" color series. Besides black, the five basic colors available were white, beige, green, pink, and blue. Standard with all the sets was an adjustable volume control for the bell. An improved, more flexible neoprene jacketed telephone cord replaced the cotton covered cords used since telephony began. As many households began using more than one phone, the telephone returned to the wall in a companion piece to the "500" desk set. The wall set was most often used in the kitchen where counter and table space was at a premium.

Mustardy Fried Chicken Breasts

4 chicken breasts
½ teaspoon salt
Dash of black pepper
1 egg
2 tablespoons prepared mustard
¼ cup grated Parmesan cheese
¼ cup bread crumbs
2 tablespoons oil
1 green bell pepper, seeded, sliced for garnish
Parsley sprig for garnish

Wipe chicken breasts with damp paper towel. Sprinkle with salt and pepper. In a bowl, beat egg and mustard together. In separate bowl, combine Parmesan cheese and bread crumbs, mixing well. Dip each chicken breast in egg mixture, then roll in cheese mixture until evenly coated. Lay chicken on wax paper and allow coating to set, about 10 minutes. Sauté chicken on both sides in heated oil 15–20 minutes, or until chicken is tender. Arrange on serving platter. Scatter green pepper slices and parsley sprig over breasts.

(Country Favorites)

Honey Mustard Chicken

4 boneless, skinless chicken breast halves
Salt and pepper to taste
2 large cloves garlic, pressed
1 teaspoon crumbled thyme
1 (20-ounce) can pineapple slices, drained, reserve juice
1 tablespoon cornstarch
¼ cup honey
¼ cup Dijon mustard

Sprinkle chicken with salt and pepper to taste. Rub with garlic and thyme. Brown in hot oil in nonstick skillet. Combine 2 tablespoons reserved juice with cornstarch. Combine honey and mustard; stir into skillet with remaining juice. Spoon sauce over chicken. Cover and simmer 15 minutes. Stir cornstarch mixture into pan juices; add pineapple slices. Cook, stirring, until sauce boils and thickens. Serves 4.

(Country Favorites)

Sweet-Sour Chicken

1 (2½- to 3-pound) broiler-fryer chicken, cut up
¾ stick butter
¼ cup firmly packed brown sugar
2 tablespoons cornstarch
½ teaspoon salt
¼ cup vinegar
1 tablespoon soy sauce
2 (8-ounce) cans pineapple chunks, drained, reserve syrup
1 cup green bell pepper strips
¼ cup thinly sliced onion
Hot cooked, buttered rice

Brown chicken in butter in large skillet. Cover; simmer 35–40 minutes; remove chicken; set aside. Combine sugar, cornstarch, and salt in skillet; gradually stir in vinegar, soy sauce, and reserved pineapple syrup. Cook over medium heat, stirring constantly, until thickened. Add pineapple, green pepper, onion, and reserved chicken. Cover and simmer 5–10 minutes. Serve over rice. Makes 4 servings.

(Cookins for Gulf Coast Council / Blue)

Ranch Chicken Breasts with Salsa

½ cup Miracle Whip salad dressing
½ cup Kraft Ranch dressing
¼–½ teaspoon ground red pepper (optional)
6 boneless, skinless chicken breast halves
Salsa

Mix dressings and pepper. Spread mixture over chicken; cover. Refrigerate at least 20 minutes to marinate. Heat grill. Remove chicken from marinade; place on grill over medium coals. Grill, covered, 8–10 minutes on each side, or until cooked through. Serve with salsa.

Variation: Omit grilling; heat broiler; place chicken on rack of broiler pan. Broil 5–7 inches from heat 8–10 minutes on each side, or until cooked through.

(Country Favorites)

Chicken Marengo

3 pounds chicken pieces
3 tablespoons shortening
1 (10¾-ounce) can tomato soup
1 (10¾-ounce) can golden mushroom soup
1 pound small whole white onions
1 medium garlic clove, minced

In large skillet, brown chicken in shortening; pour off fat. Stir in remaining ingredients; cover and cook over low heat 45 minutes, or until tender. Stir now and then. Uncover and cook until desired consistency. Serves 6–8.

Pamela White (Recipes to Remember)

Chicken Chablis

⅓ cup all-purpose flour
1 teaspoon salt
½ teaspoon pepper
2 chickens, cut in pieces
4 tablespoons butter or margarine
1 (8-ounce) can mushrooms with juice
Extra flour for thickening
Chablis wine
Half-and-half

Put flour, salt, and pepper in bag. Shake chicken pieces, a few at a time, to coat. Brown in melted butter on both sides; cover and simmer 45 minutes. Remove from pan. To juices in pan, add mushrooms and juice and enough flour to thicken like a paste. Add Chablis to make a heavy gravy. Just before serving, add 2–3 tablespoons half-and-half. Serves 8–10.

Margaret Morse (Recipes to Remember)

Delectable Chicken

1 (2½- to 3-pound) chicken, cut into serving pieces
Salt and pepper to taste
2 tablespoons butter
1 envelope beef-flavor mushroom mix
¾ cup water
2 medium tomatoes, peeled, seeded, chopped
2 tablespoons lemon juice
1 clove garlic, crushed
¼ teaspoon oregano

Preheat oven to 350°. Sprinkle chicken with salt and pepper. In large skillet, melt butter; brown chicken. Remove to 2-quart baking dish. To butter remaining in skillet, stir in soup mix, water, tomatoes, lemon juice, garlic, and oregano. Cook over medium heat, stirring occasionally, 5 minutes. Pour over chicken; bake, covered, about 1 hour, or until chicken is fork-tender. Makes about 6 servings.

Betty Yonker (Cookins for Gulf Coast Council / Red)

Detroit, Michigan, was the first city in the nation to assign individual telephone numbers in 1879.

Chicken Piccata

Handful of mushrooms
½ cup butter
½ teaspoon to 1 ounce chicken base
8–12 ounces heavy whipping cream
½ ounce white wine
2 drops lemon juice
2 chicken breasts
Flour
Oil

Cook mushrooms in butter until done, approximately 1 minute; drain. Add chicken base and cream; stir in white wine and lemon juice; cook until thick. Dredge chicken breasts in flour and cook in oil till done; drain. Add breasts to cream sauce and simmer till tender. Serves 2–4.

Mitzi King (Our Favorite Recipes)

Lillian's Chicken Casserole

½ pound bacon
2 cups Uncle Ben's raw rice
4–6 boneless, skinless chicken breasts
Salt, pepper, and garlic powder to taste
1 cup chopped onion
1 cup chopped celery
2 (10¾-ounce) cans cream of chicken soup
4 cans hot water

Line roasting pan with bacon; sprinkle rice over bacon. Lay chicken breasts on top of rice; lightly sprinkle with salt, pepper, and garlic powder. Add onion and celery to chicken soup and water; mix well. Pour over chicken. Seal with foil tightly. Bake at 350° for 2 hours on bottom rack of oven. Makes a lot.

Karen Strickland (Recipes to Remember)

Hot Chicken Casserole

2 cups diced cooked chicken
1 cup chopped celery
2 tablespoons grated onion
1 tablespoon lemon juice
½ cup mayonnaise
1 (10¾-ounce) can cream of mushroom soup
½ cup sliced almonds
1 (8-ounce) can sliced water chestnuts
1 (8-ounce) can sliced mushrooms
1 cup grated Cheddar cheese
1 cup crushed potato chips

Mix all ingredients except cheese and chips together. Put in 9x13-inch pan. Sprinkle with cheese and cover with potato chips. Bake at 450° for 15–20 minutes. Serves 6–8.

(Country Favorites)

Florentine Chicken Loaf

2 (10-ounce) packages frozen chopped spinach
3 egg whites
1 medium onion, chopped
1 tablespoon chopped parsley
1 green bell pepper, chopped
1 tablespoon garlic powder
Black pepper to taste
1 tablespoon butter
1 pound raw boneless, skinless chicken breasts, ground

Thaw spinach; drain, and blot with paper towels. Beat egg whites; combine all ingredients. Spray 5x9-inch loaf pan with cooking spray. Form mixture in pan and bake at 350° for 45–50 minutes. Remove and serve.

Jackie Rodewald (Our Favorite Recipes)

Italian Chicken Mexican Roll-Ups

4 boneless, skinless chicken breasts
1 package Italian seasoning
½ cup water
1 (8-ounce) package fat-free cream cheese, softened
1 (10¾-ounce) can cream of mushroom soup
8 flour or corn tortillas

Cook chicken, Italian seasoning, and water for 4 hours in crockpot on HIGH. Add cream cheese and soup. Cook 2 more hours. Take out chicken and shred. Divide chicken between tortillas, placing in center. Add 1 tablespoon sauce to each and roll up. Place in 9x13-inch casserole dish, seam side down. Pour rest of sauce on top. Cover with foil and bake 30 minutes at 350°. Serves 4.

Betty Hatcher (Our Favorite Recipes)

Chicken Lunch

1 (12-ounce) can white meat chicken
1 (10¾-ounce) can cream of chicken soup
½ cup milk
1 medium onion, chopped
1 (10-ounce) can tomatoes and chiles
1 cup crushed Doritos
1 cup grated cheese

Mix first 5 ingredients together in 6x11-inch glass baking dish. Sprinkle Doritos on top; cover with grated cheese and bake at 350° for 30 minutes. Serves 4–6.

Nancy Westbrook (Our Favorite Recipes)

King Ranch Chicken Casserole

1 (10¾-ounce) can cream of chicken soup
1 (10¾-ounce) can cream of mushroom soup
2 cups chicken broth
1 (10-ounce) can Ro-Tel tomatoes
12 flour tortillas, cut in pieces
1 (3- to 4-pound) chicken, cooked, cut into bite-size pieces
1 large onion, chopped
2 cups grated American cheese

Combine soups, chicken broth, and tomatoes; set aside. Oil a 3-quart casserole. Layer half of tortilla pieces, half of chicken, half of onion, and half of cheese in casserole. Pour half of chicken broth mixture over layers; repeat layers. Pour remaining chicken broth over; top with remaining cheese. Bake at 350° for 45–60 minutes. This can be frozen and reheated and will still taste great. Serves 8–10.

(Recipes to Remember)

Pepsi Chicken

1 stick margarine
1 chicken, cut up
1 (8-ounce) can Pepsi
1 (20-ounce) bottle ketchup
Salt and pepper to taste

Melt margarine in electric skillet. Place chicken pieces in skillet and pour Pepsi and ketchup over; season to taste. Cook at 225° for 2 hours. Serves 4–6.

(Country Favorites)

Chicken Croquettes

3 tablespoons butter
3 tablespoons all-purpose flour
½ teaspoon salt
1 teaspoon chili powder
1 cup scalded milk
1 cup diced chicken
4 tablespoons minced parsley
1 egg, beaten
Bread or cracker crumbs

Melt butter; add flour and seasonings; gradually add scalded milk, stirring until smooth. Cook until thick and smooth. Add diced chicken and minced parsley; cool; shape. Dip in beaten egg; roll in finely sifted bread or cracker crumbs. Fry in deep fat at 365° until well browned. Drain on absorbent paper. Serve with cream peas or chili sauce. Serves 4.

(Country Favorites)

Beer Can Chicken

½ can beer per chicken
2 tablespoons Worcestershire per ½ can beer
Whole chicken
Juice of lime, lemon, or orange
Garlic powder to taste
Salt and pepper to taste

In each ½ can beer add 2 tablespoons Worcestershire and juice of one citrus. Season chicken on outside with garlic powder and salt and pepper to taste. Insert beer can in chicken cavity; place in pie pan. Cut top of lemon or lime and place on top of chicken. Place in 350° oven for about an hour, checking periodically for doneness. May cook on barbecue grill for about 1½ hours directly on grill without pie pan.

Dale Hart (Our Favorite Recipes)

Curried Chicken and Broccoli

4 chicken breasts, or whole chicken
1 (10¾-ounce) can cream of chicken soup
½ cup mayonnaise
½ teaspoon fresh lemon juice
½ teaspoon curry powder
¼ cup soft bread crumbs
1 tablespoon butter, melted
1 (10-ounce) package frozen broccoli spears, cooked, drained
½ cup shredded Cheddar cheese
Freshly cooked rice

Place chicken in medium skillet; add water just to cover. Simmer until tender, 20–30 minutes; drain well. Let cool slightly; remove meat from bones.

Preheat oven to 350°. Combine next 4 ingredients in small bowl and blend well. Mix bread crumbs and butter in another bowl. Arrange broccoli in single layer in bottom of 1½-quart baking dish; cover with chicken. Pour soup mixture over. Sprinkle with bread crumbs and cheese. Bake until heated through, about 25 minutes. Serve over rice. Serves 6–8.

Leann Hall (Cookins for Gulf Coast Council / Blue)

Arroz con Pollo

(Chicken and Rice)

1–2 tablespoons oil
2 cups rice
½ (8-ounce) can tomato sauce
¼ onion, chopped
½ green bell pepper, chopped
2 cups chicken broth
2 cups water
¼ teaspoon crushed cumin seeds
⅛ teaspoon garlic
Salt and pepper to taste
1 whole fryer, boiled, deboned, pulled apart
1 small potato, peeled, sliced (optional)
3 small carrots, peeled, sliced (optional)
1 package dried shrimp (optional)

In large 2-quart pot, heat oil. Brown rice in oil, stirring occasionally. Add tomato sauce, onion, green pepper, chicken broth, water, seasonings, and chicken; stir well. Place potato, carrots, and shrimp on top, if desired. Bring to a boil, then reduce heat and simmer until rice is done, about 20 minutes.

Mary Davis (Our Favorite Recipes)

The coin-operated pay telephone was patented by William Gray of Hartford, Connecticut, in 1889.

Chickaritos

- 3 cups finely chopped cooked chicken
- 1 (4-ounce) can diced green chiles
- ½ cup finely chopped green onions
- 1½ cups shredded sharp Cheddar cheese
- 1 teaspoon hot pepper sauce
- 1 teaspoon garlic salt
- ¼ teaspoon pepper
- ¼ teaspoon ground cumin
- 1 (17¼-ounce) box frozen puff pastry sheets, thawed, or pie pastry for double crust
- Water
- Paprika
- Salsa and guacamole

In bowl, combine chicken, chiles, onions, cheese, and seasonings. Mix well; chill till ready to use.

Remove half the pastry from refrigerator at a time. On a lightly floured board, roll to a 9x12-inch rectangle. Cut into 9 small rectangles. Place about 2 tablespoons of filling across center of each rectangle. Wet edges of pastry with water and roll pastry around filling. Crimp edges with fork to seal. Place seam side down on a lightly greased cookie sheet. Sprinkle with paprika. Bake at 425° for 20–25 minutes, or until golden brown. Serve with salsa and guacamole. Makes 18 appetizers or 6–8 main-dish servings.

(Country Favorites)

Chicken and Bean Burritos

2 (16-ounce) cans refried beans
1 tablespoon chili powder
12 (10-inch) flour tortillas
½ cup sour cream
2 cups shredded cooked chicken
2 large tomatoes, chopped
2 cups shredded Cheddar cheese
Melted margarine (optional)
Hot or mild taco sauce

Combine beans and chili powder; set aside. Wrap stack of tortillas in foil; bake at 350° for 15 minutes to soften. Keep tortillas wrapped while preparing each burrito. Spoon ¼ cup bean mixture and a little sour cream into a strip near center of each tortilla, leaving 1-inch border at top and bottom. Arrange chicken, tomatoes, and cheese over beans and sour cream. Fold sides over filling and roll up from bottom. Serve now or place burritos, seam side down, on cookie sheet and brush with melted margarine. Bake at 375° for 15 minutes. Serve with taco sauce. Serves 6.

Carol Patterson (Cookins for Gulf Coast Council / Red)

Chicken Sopa or Chicken Enchilada Casserole

1 (10-count) package flour tortillas
1 chicken, cooked, cubed
1 (4-ounce) can chopped green chiles
1 (10¾-ounce) can cream of mushroom soup
1 (10¾-ounce) can cream of chicken soup
1 cup grated Monterey Jack cheese

Cut up tortillas into pieces and put a layer in bottom of casserole dish. Add a layer of chicken. Mix chiles and soups together and pour ½ over chicken. Repeat layers; top with cheese. Heat 40 minutes in 350° oven. Serves 4–6.

Susan Rea (Cookins for Gulf Coast Council / Red)

Enchiladas Aztecas

2 tablespoons margarine
2 tablespoons all-purpose flour
1 cup milk
1 teaspoon salt
3 cups shredded Monterey Jack cheese, divided
2 cups chopped cooked chicken
½ cup chopped avocado
⅓ cup chopped tomato
⅓ cup pitted ripe olive slices
¼ cup chopped green chile peppers
¼ cup chopped onion
12 corn tortillas
Hot oil

Make white sauce with margarine, flour, milk, and salt; add 2 cups cheese; stir till melted. Add chicken, avocado, tomato, olives, chile peppers, and onion; mix well. Dip each tortilla in hot oil to soften. Place ⅓ cup chicken mixture on each tortilla; roll up tightly. Place seam side down in oblong baking dish. Top with remaining cheese; bake at 350° for 20–25 minutes till hot. Serves 6–8.

Martha Sanford (Cookins for Gulf Coast Council / Red)

Jo's Chicken Enchiladas

3 chicken breasts
1 cup sour cream
2 (10¾-ounce) cans cream of chicken soup
1 bouillon cube dissolved in 1 soup can water
2 (4-ounce) cans chopped green chiles
2 cups shredded Cheddar cheese, divided
1 cup chopped green onions
12 corn tortillas

Cook chicken breasts in water to cover. Remove from bones and cube; reserve broth. Make sauce using sour cream, soup, water, and green chiles. Mix cheese and onions together. Dip tortillas in reserved broth to soften. Place some chicken, some sauce, and 1 tablespoon cheese mixture on each tortilla; roll up. Place in lightly greased 9x13-inch pan. Top with remaining sauce and cheese. Bake at 350° for 40–50 minutes. Doubles well. Makes 12.

Sam and Joyce Ward (Our Favorite Recipes)

Old-Fashioned Chicken and Dumplings

1 fryer, cut up
1 onion, chopped
1 tablespoon salt
¼ teaspoon pepper
6 cups water
2 cups self-rising flour
¼ teaspoon ground thyme
½ cup ice water

Combine first 5 ingredients in Dutch oven; bring to a boil. Cover and simmer until chicken is tender; remove chicken from broth. Cool and bone. Return chicken to broth and bring to a boil. Combine flour, thyme, and ice water to make a soft dough. Stir well. Turn dough out on lightly floured surface. Knead gently 30 seconds. Roll dough into ⅛-inch thickness. Cut into ½x4-inch strips. Drop strips into boiling broth. Cover and reduce heat. Simmer 30–40 minutes. Serves 6–8.

Virgia Gribble (Cookins for Gulf Coast Council / Red)

Japanese Chicken Wings

2 pounds chicken wings
½ cup soy sauce
½ cup sake
¼ cup sugar
¼ teaspoon crushed red pepper
1 garlic clove, crushed
1½ teaspoons grated fresh gingerroot

Cut chicken wings in 3 pieces (discard tips or use for soup, etc.). Mix all remaining ingredients together. Place wing parts in dish and cover with mixture. Let marinate 1 hour, turning occasionally. Cover and refrigerate 24 hours.

Bake 1½ hours at 375°. Serve warm or cold. Serves 4–6.

Virgia Gribble (Cookins for Gulf Coast Council / Red)

Easy Thanksgiving Turkey

This works for any size bird, as long as it fits in the roaster and lid fits tightly (no foil); follow instructions exactly.

1 turkey
2 stalks celery, broken
1 apple, unpeeled, cut in half
1 onion, peeled, cut in half
Salt and pepper to taste
2 sticks butter, melted
1 quart very warm water

Starting at 9:00 p.m. Thanksgiving eve, wash and clean turkey. Use a roaster with close fitting cover that bird fits into easily. Preheat oven to 475°. Place celery, apple, and onion in cavity of turkey. Salt and pepper bird to taste. Pour melted butter over bird. Add water to roaster; cover. Bake in preheated oven 1 hour. Turn off oven; do not open oven door until after 6:00 a.m. Thanksgiving morning.

You will have a tender, golden-brown turkey with lots of broth and a free oven for the rest of your day's cooking.

(Recipes to Remember)

Seafood

1959 Princess

The desk set received a smart, new look. Compactness, attractive styling, and illuminated dial (it lights up when you lift the handset, or you can keep it on as a night light) contributed to the all-around usefulness of the Princess set. Featured in a variety or colors, including pastels, its design appealed to women and teenage girls. The Princess was unique in two aspects: it required an external electric transformer to power the light-up dial, and when production began it did not contain enough room for a bell ringer, so an external ringer was required. The Princess model remained in production until 1994, with several modifications throughout the years.

With the first transcontinental microwave transmitting system now in operation, true number calling is instituted—that is, seven numerical digits without letters or names—although it took more than fifteen years to implement throughout the system. But cables provide much higher signal quality, avoid atmospheric interference, and offer greater capacity and security.

Shrimp Scampi

7 tablespoons butter
2 tablespoons crushed garlic
3 tablespoons chopped parsley
2 tablespoons lemon juice
½ teaspoon dry mustard
¼ teaspoon salt
½ cup dry white wine
2 pounds large shrimp, shelled, deveined

Melt butter in 9x13-inch pan. Add garlic, parsley, lemon juice, mustard, salt, and wine; mix well. Add shrimp and toss until well coated. Broil shrimp approximately 5 minutes on each side, or until done and lightly browned. Serve over garlic butter-flavored fettuccine.

Winnie Hutsell (Our Favorite Recipes)

Shrimp Stir-Fry

SAUCE:
½ teaspoon grated gingerroot
¼ teaspoon parsley
1 teaspoon lemon juice
½ teaspoon butter
½ teaspoon low-sodium soy sauce
2 tablespoons water
¼ teaspoon sweetener

Combine all ingredients.

2 tablespoons chopped onion
3½ ounces cooked shrimp
½ cup sliced red or green bell pepper
½ cup sliced fresh mushrooms
1 cup sliced Chinese cabbage

Spray nonstick skillet with cooking spray. Add onion, shrimp, and Sauce; simmer over medium heat 5–10 minutes. Do not cook dry. Add vegetables and stir-fry just a few minutes, until vegetables have barely cooked. Serves 4.

Jackie Rodewald (Our Favorite Recipes)

Shrimp Supreme

1 (8-ounce) package cream cheese
1 stick butter, divided
1 onion, chopped
4–5 green onions, chopped
1 teaspoon chopped garlic
1 pound peeled, deveined shrimp, or 1 pint lump crabmeat
1 teaspoon red pepper
1 teaspoon Tabasco
1 (10¾-ounce) can cream of mushroom soup
1 (4-ounce) can sliced mushrooms
Cooked rice

Melt cheese in butter (reserving 2 tablespoons) in heavy saucepan. Sauté onions and garlic in reserved butter until clear and tender; add shrimp and cook till pink. Combine all ingredients except rice in saucepan and cook about 15 minutes. Serve over rice. Serves 4.

Jean LaSalle (Cookins for Gulf Coast Council / Red)

Shrimp, Sausage, Rice Casserole

1 cup chopped celery
½ cup chopped onion
1 cup chopped green onions
½ cup butter
1 pound peeled, deveined shrimp
2 cups chopped sausage
2 cups cooked rice
1 (10¾-ounce) can cream of shrimp soup
2 (10¾-ounce) cans cream of mushroom soup, divided

Cook celery, onion, and green onions in butter till soft. Add shrimp and sausage; cook about 15 minutes. In large bowl, add cooked rice, shrimp mixture, cream of shrimp soup, and 1 can cream of mushroom soup; mix well. Pour into large casserole dish; top with remaining can cream of mushroom soup; bake at 350° for 30 minutes. Serves 6–8.

Brenda Greene (Cookins For Gulf Coast Council / Blue)

Fried Shrimp

1 egg
1 cup evaporated milk
3 cups cold water
2 pounds fresh shrimp, peeled (leave tails), deveined
Salt, black pepper, and cayenne to taste
1 cup all-purpose flour
3 cups bread crumbs

Mix egg, evaporated milk, and cold water; set aside. Slit each shrimp ¾ of its length and season generously with salt, pepper, and cayenne. Dip each shrimp in egg batter and then in flour. Dip in egg batter again and roll in bread crumbs. Fry in deep fat at 375° for 3–4 minutes. Serves 4.

Donna Wilcox (Cookins for Gulf Coast Council / Red)

Baked Herb Shrimp

½ cup margarine, melted
¼ teaspoon lemon juice
¼ teaspoon garlic salt
½ teaspoon Tabasco
½ teaspoon basil
½ teaspoon thyme
1 pound raw deveined, shelled shrimp
Paprika

Combine margarine, lemon juice, garlic salt, Tabasco, basil, and thyme; simmer 2–3 minutes. Spread shrimp in 9x13-inch glass baking dish; pour sauce over. Sprinkle with paprika; bake in 350° oven 25 minutes. Serves 4.

Tiny Ponder (Cookins for Gulf Coast Council / Red)

Shrimp Beer Batter

1 cup pancake mix
1 cup beer
1 egg
1 pound peeled, deveined shrimp

Mix pancake mix, beer, and egg. Dry shrimp on paper towels; dip in batter. Deep-fry until golden brown.

(Cookins for Gulf Coast Council / Red)

Shrimp Victoria

1 pound raw Texas shrimp, peeled, deveined
½ cup finely chopped onion
¼ cup margarine
1 (6-ounce) can sliced mushrooms, drained
1 cup sour cream
¼ teaspoon salt
Dash of cayenne pepper
1 tablespoon flour
1½ cups cooked rice

Sauté shrimp and onion in margarine 10 minutes, or until shrimp are tender. Add mushrooms, sour cream, salt, and pepper; cook 5 minutes more. Sprinkle in flour, allowing mixture to boil. Serve over rice. Makes 4–6 servings.

D. McGaughey (Cookins for Gulf Coast Council / Red)

Delicious and Easy Microwave Shrimp

2 sticks margarine
1½ tablespoons Worcestershire
2 tablespoons red pepper sauce
1½ pounds unpeeled shrimp
A1 Steak Sauce
2 tablespoons barbecue sauce

Melt margarine on MEDIUM-HIGH in 9x11-inch microwave-safe dish. Add Worcestershire and red pepper sauce. Season shrimp thoroughly with steak sauce. Combine shrimp with margarine and sauces. Cover with wax paper; cook in microwave on HIGH for 15–17 minutes, depending on size of shrimp.

(Cookins for Gulf Coast Council / Red)

Shrimp Creole

1 pound raw shrimp
2 tablespoons butter
1 cup chopped onions
½ clove garlic, chopped
⅛ teaspoon paprika
1 pint stewed tomatoes
1 cup chopped green bell pepper
Salt and pepper

Peel, wash, and devein shrimp. Melt butter and stir in onion, green pepper, and garlic. Let simmer until peppers are tender, then add tomatoes and seasoning. Boil 5 minutes. Add shrimp to this and boil 10 minutes longer.

Ray Calvo (Cookins for Gulf Coast Council / Red)

Crab Legs Almondine

1 pint water
3 eggs
Salt and pepper to taste
King crab legs, boiled, removed from shells
Flour
1 cup bread crumbs
Oil
Melted lemon butter
Sliced almonds

Whip water with eggs and seasonings. Dip crab legs into mixture, then roll in flour. Dip again into egg mixture, then roll in bread crumbs. Fry in hot deep oil until golden brown. Serve topped with lemon butter and sliced almonds. Makes 4 portions.

Johnnie Johnson (Cookins for Gulf Coast Council / Red)

Crabmeat Casserole

1 cup chopped onion
2 cups chopped celery
1 large green bell pepper, chopped
3 cloves garlic, minced
1 tablespoon oil
3 cups lump crabmeat (can use part cut-up shrimp)
1 cup Italian bread crumbs, divided
2 eggs, beaten
6 tablespoons margarine, melted
2 teaspoons chopped parsley

Sauté onion, celery, green pepper, and garlic in oil on low till transparent. Add crabmeat and ½ bread crumbs to mixture. Fold in beaten eggs. Place in baking dish; spread margarine on top. Sprinkle with remaining ½ cup bread crumbs and parsley. Bake at 350° for 30 minutes, or until top browns. Serves 5.

Bertha Myers (Cookins for Gulf Coast Council / Red)

Crab Imperial

½ cup mayonnaise
1 tablespoon Worcestershire
2 tablespoons finely chopped green bell pepper
1 (2-ounce) jar chopped pimento
½ teaspoon dry mustard
½ teaspoon salt and freshly ground pepper
1½ cups bread crumbs, divided
1 egg
1 pound lump crabmeat
¼ cup butter, melted

Mix mayonnaise, Worcestershire, green pepper, pimento, mustard, salt, black pepper, and 1 cup bread crumbs. Stir in egg and crabmeat. Put in shells or dish and sprinkle with remaining bread crumbs; cover with butter. Bake at 350° for 20–30 minutes. Serves 4–6.

Ivy Pickett (Cookins for Gulf Coast Council / Blue)

Crab Rolls

1 pound crabmeat, cut fine
1 cup Pepperidge Farm dressing mix
1 egg, beaten
1 teaspoon Worcestershire
Dried onion flakes to taste
Dried parsley flakes to taste
1 tablespoon mayonnaise
Bread crumbs

Mix all ingredients except bread crumbs; chill. Form into patties; roll in bread crumbs and fry.

Helen Thiel (Cookins for Gulf Coast Council / Blue)

Crab Casserole

¼ cup chopped onion
½ cup chopped celery
Oil
2 cups cooked crabmeat
½ cup cracker crumbs
1 egg, beaten
Salt and pepper to taste
Cornmeal to sprinkle

Cook onion and celery until soft in small amount of oil. Mix crabmeat, cracker crumbs, and egg with onion and celery. Place in greased baking dish; season to taste; sprinkle cornmeal on top. Bake at 350° for 35 minutes.

Norvell Ball (Cookins for Gulf Coast Council / Red)

Stuffed Crab and Rice Shells

¼ cup chopped onion
¼ cup chopped green bell pepper
1 clove garlic, minced
2 tablespoons margarine
3 cups cooked rice
1 (12-ounce) package crabmeat
1 cup sour cream
2 tablespoons lemon juice
2 tablespoons minced pimento
1 teaspoon parsley flakes
½ teaspoon salt
1 cup soft bread crumbs
2 tablespoons margarine, melted

Sauté onion, green pepper, and garlic in margarine till tender. Combine with rice, crabmeat, sour cream, lemon juice, pimento, parsley flakes, and salt. Divide mixture among 4 large seafood shells. Toss bread crumbs with melted margarine; sprinkle over rice mixture. Bake at 425° for 15 minutes. Serves 4.

Carol Patterson (Cookins for Gulf Coast Council / Red)

Crabmeat Stuffed Eggplant

1 (1½- to 2-pound) eggplant
1 quart plus ¼ cup water, divided
2 tablespoons butter
1 medium onion, chopped fine
2 tablespoons chopped celery
1 clove garlic, mashed
2 tablespoons cooking oil
2 slices very stale bread, soaked in ½ cup milk
½ teaspoon cayenne pepper
Pinch of oregano
Pinch of thyme
Salt and pepper to taste
½ shell of beaten egg
4 tablespoons cracker crumbs, divided
½ pound cooked crabmeat

Cut eggplant in half lengthwise. Cut around eggplant shell with paring knife; scoop out all pulp with a teaspoon; do not break shell; set aside. In quart of salted water, place eggplant shell, cut side down; cover and cook 10 minutes; drain. Grease around skin; place shell in shallow baking dish. Cut pulp in small pieces; place in saucepan with ¼ cup water and butter; cover and cook over very low heat 15 minutes, or until tender; stir occasionally. Uncover and cook out moisture, about 5 minutes.

In a small saucepan, cook onion, celery, and garlic in oil until tender, about 5 minutes, stirring constantly; add soaked bread, cook, and stir until glossy. Add cooked eggplant; stir well. Season with cayenne, oregano, thyme, and salt and pepper to taste; set aside. When cool, add beaten egg, 2 tablespoons cracker crumbs, and crabmeat; season again if needed. Spoon mixture into shells; sprinkle with remaining 2 tablespoons cracker crumbs. Preheat oven to 350°; bake 20 minutes. Flavor will improve, however, if stuffed eggplant is chilled several hours before baking. Serves 2.

Carolyn Russell (Cookins for Gulf Coast Council / Red)

Salmon Patties

2 cups salmon, drained, bone and skin removed
2 eggs, beaten
½ cup chopped onion
½ teaspoon red pepper
1 teaspoon black pepper
2 teaspoons salt
1 teaspoon Worcestershire
1 tablespoon lemon juice
1 cup all-purpose flour
½ cup oil

Mix salmon with eggs, onion, peppers, salt, and Worcestershire. Make into 8 small patties. Sprinkle with lemon juice. Roll in flour and fry in oil until brown on both sides, turning only once. Serves 4.

(Country Favorites)

Crisp Salmon Balls

1 (15-ounce) can salmon
1 egg
½ cup all-purpose flour
1 heaping teaspoon baking powder
Salt and pepper to taste

Drain salmon; save liquid; remove skin and bones. Mix salmon with egg; add flour. Mix ¼ cup of salmon liquid with baking powder slowly (it will foam). Pour into salmon mixture. Season to taste. Drop by teaspoons in hot oil and fry till brown. Makes 4–6.

Leann Hall (Cookins for Gulf Coast Council / Blue)

Honey Grilled Salmon

1–2 pounds salmon fillet

MARINADE:

1 teaspoon ground ginger
1 teaspoon garlic powder
⅓ cup soy sauce
⅓ cup orange juice
¼ cup honey

Place salmon fillet in zipper bag and pour Marinade over, reserving small amount for basting. Place in refrigerator at least 4 hours.

Lightly grease grill. Grill 12–15 minutes per side, or until done. Brush on additional Marinade while cooking. Serves 2.

Dale Hart (Our Favorite Recipes)

Sour Cream Salmon Puffs

1 (15½-ounce) can salmon, drained
1½ cups soft bread crumbs
1 (8-ounce) container sour cream
2 eggs, separated
2 tablespoons chopped chives
¼ teaspoon salt
Dash of pepper
1¼ cups finely chopped almonds
Vegetable oil
Lemon wedges

Remove skin and bones from salmon. In large bowl, combine salmon, crumbs, sour cream, egg yolks, chives, salt, and pepper; mix well. Beat egg whites until stiff; fold into salmon mixture. On large sheet of wax paper, sprinkle half the almonds. Drop heaping tablespoonfuls of salmon mixture onto almonds; sprinkle remaining almonds over top. In large skillet, heat oil; lift puffs with spatula into skillet. Brown on each side. Serve hot with lemon wedges.

Carol Patterson (Cookins for Gulf Coast Council / Red)

Baked Red Snapper

1 (4-pound) red snapper
Creole seasoning to taste
2 sticks margarine, melted
1 cup chopped onion
1 cup chopped celery
½ cup chopped green bell pepper
4 cloves garlic, minced
1 (8-ounce) can tomato sauce
1 teaspoon sugar
1 tablespoon Worcestershire
¼ cup dry white wine

Season fish inside and out with Creole seasoning; place in open baking pan. Make sauce with margarine, vegetables, tomato sauce, sugar, and Worcestershire; cook over low heat till vegetables are tender. Pour wine over red snapper, then pour sauce over. Place in 300° oven; cook 1 hour, basting occasionally. Serves 8.

Carolyn Russell (Cookins for Gulf Coast Council / Red)

In the early days, operators working at a large switchboard would answer an incoming telephone call and connect it manually to the party being called. The first automatic telephone exchange was patented by Almon Strowger of Kansas City in 1891 and installed in 1892, but manual switchboards remained in common use. The last manual switchboard in the Southern Bell region was removed from service in Rosedale, Mississippi, on September 21, 1969.

Stuffed Flounder

2 medium-size flounders, cleaned
Creole seasoning, divided
¼ cup butter
1 small onion, chopped
1 medium green bell pepper, chopped
1 cup diced celery
7 slices bread
1 cup chopped green onions
½ cup chopped parsley
½ pound fresh crabmeat
Paprika
Juice of 1 lemon

Slit a pocket in flounders for stuffing. Season inside and out with Creole seasoning. Melt butter in skillet; add onion, bell pepper, and celery. Simmer until wilted. Soak bread in water; squeeze water from bread. Break up in pieces and add to skillet. Add green onions, parsley, crabmeat, additional Creole seasoning, and paprika; cover skillet and cook on low about 15 minutes. Fill flounders with stuffing. Place in shallow pan in 350° oven for 40–50 minutes. Baste with lemon juice and pan drippings. Serves 2.

Clayton Weeks (Cookins for Gulf Coast Council / Red)

The early phones didn't always have a built-in ringer; one simply whistled loudly into the telephone and hoped the person on the other end was close enough to hear it.

Crawfish Étouffée

¾ stick butter
3 tablespoons flour
1 teaspoon chopped garlic
½ teaspoon chopped shallots
1 teaspoon chopped parsley
3 cups consommé or veal stock
⅓ teaspoon paprika
1 teaspoon tomato purée
⅓ cup dry white wine
⅓ cup diced red or green bell pepper
20 ounces crawfish tails
Salt and cayenne pepper to taste

Melt butter in medium sauté pan; add flour and make a golden roux. Add garlic, shallots, and parsley; stir over reduced heat. Add consommé or veal stock, paprika, tomato purée, and white wine; stir with wire whip until smooth and thick consistency; simmer 20 minutes. Add pepper and crawfish. Add salt and cayenne pepper to taste. Cook over medium heat until everything is combined. Serve over rice. Serves 4.

Virgia Gribble (Cookins for Gulf Coast Council / Red)

Fried Frog Legs

8 frog legs
¾ cup lemon juice
¼ cup water
1 teaspoon salt, divided
½ teaspoon pepper
1 cup flour, divided
1 teaspoon baking powder
1 tablespoon sugar
1 cup milk

Marinate frog legs in lemon juice, water, ½ teaspoon salt, and pepper for 1 hour. Mix ¼ cup flour and all remaining ingredients in bowl for batter. Remove frog legs from marinade. Dip in batter, coating thoroughly. Roll in mixture of remaining flour and salt. Fry in hot fat, covered, until tender. Remove cover and brown lightly. Serves 4.

(Country Favorites)

Seafood Cocktail Sauce

1 teaspoon chili powder
2 tablespoons lemon juice
½ cup ketchup
1 tablespoon horseradish
½ teaspoon salt

Blend chili powder with lemon juice; mix other ingredients; chill. Serve over any seafood: shrimp, oysters, crabmeat, scallops, etc. Makes 1 serving.

(Country Favorites)

Cakes

1964
Touch-Tone

As America neared the 200 million mark in population, a new era in telephoning services began with push-button calling. Touch-Tone service was introduced, limiting errors and increasing the speed of dialing. A keypad replaced the familiar rotary "pulse" dial, and early Touch-Tone sets had only ten buttons. (The * and # keys were added in 1968.) The Touch-Tone system could travel across microwave transmitter links and work rapidly with solid state computer-controlled phone exchanges. A tone is produced as long as a key is depressed. No matter how long you press, the tone is decoded as the appropriate digit. The shortest duration in which a digit can be sent and decoded is about 100 milliseconds by automatic dialers. A twelve-digit long-distance phone number can be dialed by an automatic phone dialer in a little more than a second—about as long as it takes a pulse dial to send a single "0" digit.

Cinnamon Streusel Cake

1 (16-ounce) package pound cake mix
1 (3-ounce) package vanilla instant pudding mix
½ cup vegetable oil
4 eggs
½ cup water
¼ cup dark corn syrup

Combine dry ingredients in large mixing bowl. Combine liquid ingredients and add to dry ingredients; mix well.

STREUSEL:

½ cup all-purpose flour
½ cup dark brown sugar, firmly packed
2 teaspoons cinnamon
2 tablespoons butter
¾ cup chopped nuts

Blend together flour, brown sugar, and cinnamon. Cut in butter with pastry blender; add nuts. Sprinkle ⅓ mixture followed by ⅓ batter into generously greased but not floured 10-cup fluted microwave-safe baking dish or Bundt-shaped pan; repeat layers of Streusel and batter twice.

Bake in microwave oven on MEDIUM for 15 minutes, turning 1–3 times during cooking, or until top springs back when lightly pressed with finger. Let stand 10 minutes; remove and invert onto serving platter.

Susan Rea (Cookins for Gulf Coast Council / Blue)

Sock-It-To-Me Cake

1 (18¼-ounce) package butter cake mix
½ cup sugar
⅔ cup Crisco oil
1 cup sour cream
4 eggs
1 teaspoon vanilla
3 tablespoons brown sugar
1½ teaspoons cinnamon
½ cup chopped nuts

Mix cake mix, sugar, oil, sour cream, eggs, and vanilla. Pour ⅓ mixture in greased and floured tube pan. Mix brown sugar, cinnamon, and nuts and sprinkle over cake batter; top with remaining cake batter. Bake at 350° for 1 hour.

ICING:

1 cup powdered sugar
1 teaspoon vanilla
2 tablespoons milk
1 tablespoon hot melted butter

Combine ingredients and drizzle over cake while still warm.

Variation: Instead of brown sugar mixture, add ¼ cup poppy seeds to cake mixture and mix well. Also, instead of using flour for dusting tube pan, use sugar and then no icing.

Esther Hays (Cookins for Gulf Coast Council / Blue)

Fresh Apple Cake

CAKE:

2 cups sugar
1 cup shortening
4 eggs
3 cups all-purpose flour
1 teaspoon cinnamon
1 teaspoon allspice
1 teaspoon cloves
1 teaspoon baking soda, dissolved in ½ cup water
4 or 5 apples, peeled, sliced fine

Cream sugar and shortening; add eggs, one at a time; beat well. Sift flour and spices; add water-soda mixture gradually; add to creamed mixture, and mix well. Fold in apples. Bake in 3 (9-inch) greased and floured pans at 350° for 30–35 minutes.

FROSTING:

3 tablespoons all-purpose flour
1 cup sugar
2 eggs
1 cup milk
1 teaspoon vanilla
1 cup chopped pecans

In saucepan, mix flour and sugar. Beat eggs by hand; add to milk. Mix into flour and sugar slowly until smooth. Cook slowly until mixture thickens; stir constantly to avoid scorching. Add vanilla and pecans; mix and cool. Spread over cake layers, then assemble cake and frost sides.

Louise Kosub (Our Favorite Recipes)

Strawberry Cake

1 (18¼-ounce) box white cake mix
½ (10-ounce) package frozen strawberries (reserve rest for Icing)
4 eggs
⅓ cup oil
1 (3-ounce) box strawberry Jell-O, dissolved in ½ cup warm water

Mix all ingredients; bake in 3 (9-inch) cake pans or 1 tube pan at 325° for 25–30 minutes.

ICING:

Reserved ½ package strawberries
1 (1-pound) box powdered sugar
⅔ cup butter, softened

Combine ingredients and spread on warm cake.

Regina Sherman (Cookins for Gulf Coast Council / Red)

Mandarin Orange Cake

2 eggs
2 (11-ounce) cans Mandarin oranges, well drained
2 cups all-purpose flour
2 teaspoons baking soda
½ teaspoon salt

Beat eggs; add oranges. Sift dry ingredients together and add to mixture; beat 4 minutes with electric mixer. Pour into greased and floured 9x13-inch pan. Bake at 350° for 30–35 minutes.

ICING:

¾ cup brown sugar
3 tablespoons milk
2 tablespoons butter
Whipped topping (optional)

Bring sugar, milk, and butter to a boil; remove from heat. Pour over hot cake as soon as it comes from the oven. When cool, serve with whipped topping, if desired.

Marlene Abraham (Cookins for Gulf Coast Council / Red)

Orange Kiss-Me Cake

1 orange, reserve ½ cup juice
1 cup raisins
⅓ cup walnuts
2 cups all-purpose flour, fill lightly and level off
1 teaspoon baking soda
1 cup sugar
1 teaspoon salt
1 cup milk
½ cup shortening
2 eggs

Heat oven to 350°. Grease and flour 9x13-inch pan. Grind orange peel and pulp, raisins, and walnuts together; set aside. In large bowl, blend flour, soda, sugar, salt, milk, shortening, and eggs; beat 3 minutes at medium speed. Stir in orange-raisin mixture. Pour into prepared pan; bake at 350° for 35–40 minutes.

TOPPING:

⅓ cup reserved orange juice
⅓ cup sugar
1 teaspoon cinnamon
¼ cup finely chopped walnuts
Orange slices for garnish

Drizzle orange juice over warm cake. Combine sugar, cinnamon, and walnuts; sprinkle over cake. If desired, garnish with orange slices. Serves 12–15.

(Country Favorites)

Peach Dump Cake

2 (16-ounce) or 1 (29-ounce) can peaches in heavy syrup
1 (18¼-ounce) box yellow cake mix
¾ cup butter, melted
½ teaspoon ground cinnamon

Layer each ingredient, without mixing, in greased 9x13-inch baking pan. Bake at 375° for 45 minutes.

For a buttery flavor, add a few squares of butter to top of cake before it cools.

Sylvia Vasquez (Recipes to Remember)

Apricot Nectar Cake

1 (18¼-ounce) package yellow cake mix
1 (3-ounce) package lemon Jell-O
½ cup Wesson oil
1 cup apricot nectar
4 eggs
1 teaspoon lemon extract

Mix together cake mix, Jell-O, oil, and apricot nectar. Add eggs, one at a time; mix well. Add lemon extract. Pour into greased and floured Bundt pan and bake at 350° for 55–60 minutes. Serves 16.

½ cup apricot nectar
¼ teaspoon lemon extract
½ cup sugar

In saucepan, mix all ingredients; bring to a boil. Pour over hot cake.

Leon Beach (Cookins for Gulf Coast Council / Blue)

Lemon Cake

1 cup plus 2 tablespoons butter, softened
2¼ cups sugar
6 eggs, separated, room temperature
3¼ cups all-purpose flour
1 tablespoon baking powder
1 cup plus 2 tablespoons milk
¾ teaspoon lemon juice

Cream butter; gradually add sugar. Add egg yolks, one at a time. Combine flour and baking powder; add to butter mixture alternately with milk. Stir in lemon juice. Beat egg whites until stiff peaks form; fold into batter. Bake at 350° for 45–55 minutes.

ICING:
½ cup butter, softened
1 teaspoon lemon extract
2–3 tablespoons lemon juice
1 (1-pound) box powdered sugar

Blend butter, lemon extract, and juice, and half of sugar; mix well. Beat in remaining sugar, adding just enough to make smooth frosting. Drizzle over edges of cake.

Barbara Wilson (Our Favorite Recipes)

The dial telephone was invented by Almon Strowger of St. Louis, Missouri, who patented the automatic telephone exchange in 1891. Mr. Strowger, a mortician, developed the method of direct dialing because he felt exchange operators were diverting his business calls to his competitors. The dial phone was not put into service until 1905 when Dial Switching Equipment was developed. Now, all of this switching equipment has been replaced by computer circuitry.

Lemon Jell-O Cake

1 (18¼-ounce) package lemon cake mix
⅔ cup water
⅔ cup oil
1 lemon, grated
1 (3-ounce) package lemon Jell-O
4 eggs
1 teaspoon lemon extract

Mix all ingredients, beating until smooth. Bake in greased tube pan 55 minutes at 325°.

ICING:
Juice of 1 lemon
1 cup powdered sugar
4 tablespoons margarine

Heat ingredients till sugar is dissolved; pour over cake before it cools.

Marguerite Singleton (Cookins for Gulf Coast Council / Blue)

No Bake Fruit Cake

1 box vanilla wafers, crumbled
1 (14-ounce) can condensed milk
1 cup raisins
1 (3-ounce) jar red cherries, drained
1 (3-ounce) jar green cherries, drained
2 cups chopped nuts
1 (16-ounce) bag flaked coconut

Combine all ingredients in large bowl; mix well. Pat into 9x9-inch pan lined with wax paper. Let sit 4 or more hours in refrigerator before cutting.

Joyce Kilbourn (Recipes to Remember)

Banana Pudding Cake

CAKE:

1 (18¼-ounce) package yellow cake mix
8 tablespoons butter, melted
1 cup whole milk
3 large eggs
1 teaspoon vanilla extract

Preheat oven to 350°. Spray 9x13-inch pan with vegetable cooking spray. Mix cake mix, butter, milk, eggs, and vanilla in large mixing bowl. Blend with electric mixer on low for 1 minute. Stop and scrape sides of bowl; increase mixer speed to medium and beat 2 minutes, scraping down sides again, if needed. The batter should look thick and well blended. Pour into prepared pan, smoothing out with rubber spatula. Place pan in oven; bake until golden brown and springs back in center when lightly pressed with finger (30 minutes). Remove pan from oven and place on wire rack to cool.

PUDDING:

1 (5.1-ounce) package vanilla instant pudding mix
3 cups whole milk
2 teaspoons vanilla extract
4 cups sliced bananas (about 3 large bananas)
1 (16-ounce) carton whipped topping, thawed
½ cup crushed vanilla wafer cookies

Mix pudding with milk and vanilla; fold in banana slices. Spoon Pudding and banana mixture on top of cooled Cake. Spread to cover all edges. Cover Pudding with whipped topping; sprinkle with crushed vanilla wafer cookies. Serves 12–15.

GeraLyn "Gerri" Gray (Our Favorite Recipes)

Piña Colada Cake

1 (18¼-ounce) package extra moist white cake mix
¼ cup Crisco oil
3 eggs
1 cup sour cream
1 (8½-ounce) can cream of coconut

In large bowl of electric mixer, combine cake mix, oil, eggs, sour cream, and cream of coconut; beat well. Pour into 2 greased and floured 8- or 9-inch layer cake pans. Bake at 350° for 30 minutes, or until cake springs back when lightly touched. Cool in pan 15 minutes. Remove cake from pans and cool completely on rack.

PIÑA COLADA FROSTING:

1 (8-ounce) package cream cheese, softened
1 (1-pound) box powdered sugar
1 teaspoon vanilla
1 (8-ounce) can crushed pineapple, drained, blotted dry
Angel Flake Coconut

Mix cream cheese, powdered sugar, vanilla, and pineapple. Use 1 tablespoon pineapple juice, if needed for consistency. Spread on cake layers and sprinkle with coconut.

Robbie Daw (Cookins for Gulf Coast Council / Blue)

Mom's Pineapple Upside Down Cake

BATTER:

3 eggs, separated
1 cup granulated sugar
5 tablespoons reserved pineapple juice
1 cup all-purpose flour, sifted
1 teaspoon baking powder
Pinch of salt

Beat egg yolks; add sugar and pineapple juice. Add flour, baking powder, and salt that have been sifted together. Fold in slightly beaten egg whites. Pour over Pineapple Slices in skillet. Bake 40 minutes at 350°. Cool 5–10 minutes. Place cake plate over skillet and turn over. Serve with whipped cream.

PINEAPPLE SLICES:

½ cup butter
1 cup brown sugar
6–8 slices pineapple, drained, reserve juice
2 tablespoons chopped pecans or raisins

Melt butter in medium iron skillet. Spread brown sugar over melted butter. Arrange pineapple slices on brown sugar. Drop pecans or raisins in open spaces; cover with Batter.

Debra Martin (Our Favorite Recipes)

Punch Bowl Cake

1 (18¼-ounce) box yellow cake mix
2 (3-ounce) packages French vanilla instant pudding mix
4 cups milk
2 (15-ounce) cans crushed pineapple, drained
2 (21-ounce) cans cherry pie filling
2 (12-ounce) cartons Cool Whip
½ cup chopped pecans

Bake cake as directed on box; cool. Crumble half of cake (large crumbles) into punch bowl. Mix pudding with milk according to directions; spoon half of mixture over cake. Spoon half of pineapple over pudding. Spoon half of cherry pie filling over pineapple. Spoon half of Cool Whip over pie filling. Sprinkle half of pecans over Cool Whip. Repeat layers. You may have to adjust the amounts of the first process to the size and shape of your punch bowl. Refrigerate.

Louise Kosub (Our Favorite Recipes)

Neiman Marcus Cake

FIRST LAYER:

1 (18¼-ounce) box yellow cake mix
1 stick butter, softened
1 cup flaked coconut (optional)
2 eggs
1 cup chopped pecans

Preheat oven to 350°. Spray 9x13-inch pan with cooking spray. Mix ingredients; press into pan.

SECOND LAYER:

1 (1-pound) box powdered sugar
1 tablespoon vanilla
1 (8-ounce) package cream cheese, softened

Mix ingredients with mixer for 1 minute, or until well blended. Spread on First Layer. Bake for 30 minutes.

Dolores Stone (Our Favorite Recipes)

Swedish Cake

2 cups sugar
1 (20-ounce) can crushed pineapple, undrained
1 teaspoon baking soda
1 teaspoon vanilla
2 eggs
2 cups all-purpose flour
1 cup chopped nuts

Combine all ingredients by hand. Bake in greased and floured 9x13-inch pan 35–40 minutes at 350°.

ICING:

1 stick margarine, softened
1 (8-ounce) package cream cheese, softened
1 teaspoon vanilla
½ cup chopped nuts
2 cups powdered sugar

Combine all ingredients; spread on warm cake. Keep in refrigerator overnight.

(Country Favorites)

White Texas Sheet Cake

1 cup butter
1 cup water
2 cups all-purpose flour
2 cups sugar
2 eggs, beaten
½ cup sour cream
1 teaspoon almond extract
1 teaspoon salt
1 teaspoon baking soda

In large saucepan, bring butter and water to a boil. Remove from heat; stir in flour, sugar, eggs, sour cream, almond extract, salt, and baking soda until smooth. Pour into a greased 10x15-inch baking pan; bake at 375° for 20–22 minutes, or until golden brown and tests done; cool 20 minutes. Makes 16–20 servings.

FROSTING:

½ cup butter
¼ cup milk
1 (1-pound) box confectioners' sugar
½ teaspoon almond extract
1 cup chopped walnuts

Combine butter and milk in saucepan; bring to a boil. Remove from heat; add sugar and extract; mix well. Stir in walnuts; spread over warm cake.

(Country Favorites)

Zucchini Cake

2½ cups all-purpose flour
2 cups sugar
1½ teaspoons ground cinnamon
1 teaspoon salt
½ teaspoon baking soda
1 cup vegetable oil
4 eggs, beaten
2 cups shredded zucchini
½ cup chopped walnuts or pecans

Combine flour, sugar, cinnamon, salt, and baking soda. Combine oil and eggs; add to flour mixture. Add zucchini and nuts. Pour into greased 9x13-inch baking pan. Bake at 350° for 35–40 minutes; cool.

FROSTING:

1 (3-ounce) package cream cheese, softened
½ cup butter, softened
1 tablespoon milk
1 teaspoon vanilla extract
2 cups confectioners' sugar

Combine all ingredients; mix well. Frost cake; sprinkle with additional nuts, if desired. Store in refrigerator.

Karen Strickland (Recipes to Remember)

Texas Tornado Cake

2¼ cups granulated sugar, divided
2 eggs
2 cups fruit cocktail, undrained
2 teaspoons baking soda
2 cups all-purpose flour
¼ cup brown sugar
1 cup chopped nuts
1 stick butter
½ cup evaporated milk
1 cup flaked coconut

Preheat oven to 325°. Lightly grease and flour a 9x13-inch pan. In a large bowl, mix and cream together 1½ cups sugar, eggs, fruit cocktail, baking soda, and flour with electric mixer. Pour into prepared pan.

In small bowl, combine brown sugar and nuts; sprinkle onto batter; bake 40 minutes. When cake is nearly done, melt butter in saucepan, adding remaining ¾ cup sugar and milk; boil 2 minutes, then add coconut. Spoon icing over cake as soon as cake is removed from oven. Cut into squares when cool.

Debra Kraatz (Our Favorite Recipes)

Fig Cake

2 cups all-purpose flour
1 teaspoon baking soda
1 teaspoon nutmeg
1 teaspoon cinnamon
1 cup butter, softened
1 cup sugar
3 eggs
1 cup buttermilk
1 pint homemade fig preserves, mashed
1–1½ cups chopped pecans
1 teaspoon vanilla

Sift together flour, soda, nutmeg, and cinnamon; set aside. Cream butter and sugar in mixer; add eggs 1 at a time, creaming after each. Add alternately buttermilk and flour mixture to butter mixture, ending with flour mixture. Add figs, nuts, and vanilla. Pour into a greased and floured tube pan or Bundt pan and bake 1 hour at 325°, or until cake springs back when touched lightly. Let sit a few minutes, then remove and cool on rack.

Ivy Pickett (Cookins for Gulf Coast Council / Blue)

German Chocolate Upside Down Cake

1 cup flaked coconut
1 cup chopped pecans
1 (18¼-ounce) box German chocolate cake mix
3 large eggs
1¼ cups water
¼ cup oil
1 (8-ounce) package cream cheese
½ cup margarine
1 (16-ounce) box powdered sugar

Grease a 9x13-inch pan. Line with wax paper cut to fit; grease paper. Sprinkle coconut and pecans into pan evenly; set aside. Combine cake mix, eggs, water, and oil; mix. Spoon and spread batter evenly over coconut-pecan mixture. Place cream cheese and margarine in small saucepan or microwave. Cook and stir over low heat until melted and smooth. Add sifted powdered sugar. Mix together well. Spoon evenly over cake batter. Bake at 350° for 40–50 minutes. Cool on rack 10 minutes. Invert onto a serving plate. Remove and discard wax paper.

Sam and Joyce Ward (Our Favorite Recipes)

Best Chocolate Cake Ever

CAKE:

2 cups sugar
2 cups all-purpose flour
¼ cup unsweetened cocoa
1 stick butter
1 cup water
½ cup oil
2 eggs
½ cup buttermilk
1½ teaspoons baking soda
1 teaspoon vanilla

Preheat oven to 350°. Spray 9x13-inch baking pan with cooking spray. Combine sugar, flour, and cocoa in large bowl. Melt butter with water and oil in small saucepan over medium-high heat; bring to a boil; pour over dry ingredients and mix well. Add eggs, buttermilk, baking soda, and vanilla; blend thoroughly. Pour batter into pan; bake until tester comes out clean, 20–25 minutes.

FROSTING:

1 (1-pound) box powdered sugar
1 cup chopped nuts
¼ cup unsweetened cocoa
1 stick butter
⅓ cup buttermilk
1 teaspoon vanilla

Combine powdered sugar, nuts, and cocoa in mixing bowl. Melt butter in saucepan over medium heat; add to sugar mixture with buttermilk and vanilla; blend thoroughly. Immediately pour over cake, spreading evenly to edges. Let cake cool in pan.

Dolores Stone (Cookins for Gulf Coast Council / Red)

Marshmallow Chocolate Cake

2 sticks margarine
2 cups sugar
4 tablespoons cocoa
4 eggs, beaten
1½ cups all-purpose flour
1 cup chopped nuts
2 cups miniature marshmallows

Mix all ingredients except marshmallows and pour into a greased and floured 10x14-inch pan; bake at 350° for 20–25 minutes. While warm, cover top with marshmallows; cool. Cover with Icing.

ICING:

1 (1-pound) box powdered sugar
1 stick margarine, softened
4 tablespoons cocoa
7 or 8 tablespoons milk

Combine ingredients until smooth. Spread over marshmallows. Cake will fall while cooling; that's okay.

(Cookins for Gulf Coast Council / Red)

Better Than Robert Redford Cake

FIRST LAYER:

1 heaping cup self-rising flour
1 stick butter, softened
⅔ cup chopped pecans

Mix all ingredients; pat into bottom of 9x13-inch pan. Bake 15 minutes at 375°; cool completely before adding next layer.

SECOND LAYER:

1 (8-ounce) package cream cheese, softened
1 cup powdered sugar
1 cup Cool Whip

Mix all ingredients together; spread over cooled First Layer.

THIRD LAYER:

1 (3-ounce) package chocolate instant pudding mix
1½ cups milk

Mix together well; let stand a few minutes to thicken. Spread over Second Layer.

FOURTH LAYER:

1 (3-ounce) package vanilla instant pudding mix
1½ cups milk

Mix together well; let stand a few minutes to thicken. Spread over Third Layer.

FIFTH LAYER:

1 (12-ounce) carton Cool Whip
½ cup chopped pecans

Spread Cool Whip over entire top; sprinkle with chopped pecans. Chill 2 or 3 hours until ready to serve.

Doris Owens (Cookins for Gulf Coast Council / Red)

Coco Lopez Cake

Great summer dessert!

1 (18¼-ounce) box yellow cake mix (not butter)
1 (14-ounce) package Angel Flake Coconut, divided
1 (15-ounce) can Coco Lopez Cream of Coconut
1 (12-ounce) carton Cool Whip

Mix cake as directed except add half a package of coconut to mix. Bake as directed for 9x13-inch pan. Remove cake from oven; immediately poke holes all over cake with end of wooden spoon. Shake cream of coconut and pour into holes in cake; let cool. Ice with Cool Whip and top with remaining coconut. Refrigerate and eat.

Lisa Sherrouse (Our Favorite Recipes)

Golden Westerner

3 sticks butter, softened
1 (1-pound) box powdered sugar
6 eggs, room temperature
1 pound all-purpose flour
1 teaspoon lemon juice
1 tablespoon vanilla

Cream butter; add powdered sugar and beat till fluffy. Add eggs, one at a time; beat well after each addition. Sift flour 3 times and add gradually to batter. Add lemon juice and vanilla; mix well. Bake in 10-inch greased and floured tube pan at 325° for 1½ hours. Cool 4 minutes, then invert pan. Makes a very large cake.

Variation: Amber Westerner: Use 1 pound carton brown sugar instead of powdered sugar.

JoAnn Comer (Cookins for Gulf Coast Council / Red)

Rum Cake

½ cup chopped pecans
1 (18¼-ounce) package butter recipe golden cake mix
1 (3-ounce) package vanilla instant pudding mix
½ cup light rum
½ cup water
½ cup Crisco oil
4 eggs

Grease and flour a Bundt or tube pan. Crumble nuts in bottom of pan. Place cake mix and pudding mix in large mixing bowl. Add rum, water, oil, and eggs; mix 2 minutes. Pour into cake pan and bake at 325° for 50–60 minutes. Remove cake from oven and immediately pour on Hot Rum Glaze. Hot glaze will cause cake to settle, but don't be alarmed, for the cake will taste yummy. Cool cake in pan 30 minutes; remove to serving plate.

HOT RUM GLAZE:

1 cup sugar
1 stick butter
¼ cup light rum
¼ cup water

Place ingredients in small saucepan and boil 2–3 minutes.

Lela McMakin (Cookins for Gulf Coast Council / Red)

The mobile telephone was invented by Bell Telephone Company and introduced into New York City police cars in 1924. Although the first commercial mobile telephone service became available in St. Louis, Missouri, in 1946, the mobile telephone would not become common for another four decades.

Italian Cream Cake

2 cups sugar
1 stick margarine plus ½ cup shortening, softened
5 eggs, separated
1 cup buttermilk
1 teaspoon baking soda
2 cups all-purpose flour
Vanilla
1 can flaked coconut
1 cup chopped pecans

Cream sugar, margarine, and shortening; add 1 egg yolk at a time; beat well. Mix buttermilk and baking soda; let sit for a few minutes. Add to sugar and margarine mixture alternately with flour. Add vanilla; fold in beaten egg whites, coconut, and pecans. Pour into prepared 9x13-inch baking pan; bake at 325° for 25–30 minutes. Allow to cool.

ICING:
1 stick margarine, softened
1 (8-ounce) package cream cheese, softened
1 (1-pound) box powdered sugar
1 teaspoon vanilla

Combine ingredients and beat until fluffy. Ice cake.

Hildegarde Brinkmeyer (Cookins for Gulf Coast Council / Red)

Sweet Potato Cream Cheese Cake

⅔ cup butter, softened
2 cups sugar
4 eggs, separated
1 cup mashed cooked sweet potatoes
2 cups all-purpose flour
1 teaspoon baking soda
1 teaspoon allspice
1 teaspoon cinnamon
1 teaspoon ground cloves
1 teaspoon nutmeg
1 cup buttermilk
½ teaspoon vanilla
1 (8-ounce) package cream cheese, softened
1 whole egg plus 1 egg yolk
Confectioners' sugar

Cream butter and sugar in large mixer bowl; add 4 egg yolks, mixing well. Pour in potatoes. Sift dry ingredients together and add to sugar mixture alternately with buttermilk. In separate bowl, beat 4 egg whites until stiff; fold in along with vanilla.

In another bowl, beat cream cheese with 1 whole egg and 1 egg yolk until fluffy. Grease and flour Bundt pan. Pour small amount of cake batter in bottom of pan. Pour in cream cheese mixture; then remainder of cake batter. Bake at 350° for 1 hour, or until cake tester comes out clean. Cool and sprinkle with confectioners' sugar.

Leann Hall (Cookins for Gulf Coast Council / Blue)

Sour Cream Cake

2 sticks margarine, softened
2 cups plus 2 tablespoons sugar, divided
2 eggs
2 cups all-purpose flour
1 teaspoon baking powder
½ pint sour cream
1 cup chopped pecans
1 teaspoon cinnamon

Cream together margarine, 2 cups sugar, and eggs. Sift flour and baking powder together and add to cream mixture a little at a time. Add sour cream; mix. Combine pecans, 2 tablespoons sugar, and cinnamon; sprinkle ½ mixture in bottom of greased and floured tube pan. Pour in batter; add remaining pecan mixture over top of batter; bake 1 hour at 300°.

Rita Londers (Cookins for Gulf Coast Council / Red)

Chess Pie Cake

1 (18¼-ounce) package yellow butter cake mix
4 eggs, divided
1 stick margarine, melted
1 (1-pound) box powdered sugar
1 (8-ounce) package cream cheese, softened

Mix together cake mix, 1 egg, and margarine; press into a 9x13-inch greased pan. Beat powdered sugar, cream cheese, and remaining 3 eggs until smooth. Pour over cake batter. Bake 1 hour at 300°–325°. Cool; cut into squares. Serves 15.

Note: May substitute chocolate butter cake mix for yellow cake mix.

Dorothy Page (Cookins for Gulf Coast Council / Blue)

Rich and Ravishing Cheesecake

CRUST:

1¼ cups graham cracker crumbs
¼ cup butter, melted
¼ cup sugar

Combine all ingredients; pat on bottom and sides of 9-inch springform pan.

CHEESECAKE:

5 (8-ounce) packages cream cheese, softened
1¾ cups sugar
¼ teaspoon vanilla
3 tablespoons all-purpose flour
1½ teaspoons grated orange peel
1½ teaspoons grated lemon peel
5 large eggs
2 eggs yolks
¼ cup heavy cream

Beat cream cheese, sugar, vanilla, flour, and orange and lemon peel on high until very smooth. Add eggs and egg yolks, one at a time, beating well after each. Stir in heavy cream. Pour mixture into Crust. Bake at 500° for 10 minutes; reset oven to 250° and bake 1 hour, or until center is set. Serves 16.

Mary Jane Garner (Cookins for Gulf Coast Council / Blue)

Cookies and Candies

1968
Trimline

The twelve-button Touch-Tone Trimline was dramatically different from any other phone at the time. With the first ever dial-in-handset, it allowed people to dial a new call without returning to the base of the phone. The design of the phone later paved the way for today's cordless and cellular phones. Although only ten buttons were needed for ordinary dialing, the two "extra" buttons (the * and # keys) were added for advanced services and for dialing international phone calls. The first Touch-Tone Trimline phone had round buttons instead of square. The convenience of having the dial in the handset was especially handy in the wall-mount model. The Trimline model also introduced the concept of modular plugs. Also in 1968, 911 was introduced as a nationwide emergency number.

Chocolate Dream Cookies

2 cups sugar
1 stick butter, softened
Pinch of salt
4 tablespoons cocoa
½ cup milk
1 teaspoon vanilla
1 cup flaked coconut
3 cups quick rolled oats

Put first 5 ingredients in saucepan; boil, stirring constantly, 3 minutes. Remove from heat and add remaining ingredients. Drop by tablespoonfuls onto wax paper; cool. Makes about 30.

(Country Favorites)

The Ultimate Chocolate Chip Cookie

¾ cup butter-flavor Crisco
1¼ cups firmly packed brown sugar
2 tablespoons milk
1 tablespoon vanilla
1 egg
1½ cups all-purpose flour
1 teaspoon salt
¾ teaspoon baking soda
1 cup semisweet chocolate chips
1 cup large pecan pieces

Heat oven to 375°. Combine Crisco, brown sugar, milk, and vanilla; beat 2 minutes. Add egg; beat again. Combine dry ingredients; add to mixture. Stir in chocolate and nuts. Drop by rounded teaspoonfuls onto ungreased baking sheet. Bake at 375° for 8–9 minutes. Makes 2½ dozen cookies.

Karen Strickland (Recipes to Remember)

Chunky Chocolate Cookie Mix in a Jar

Makes a nice gift.

¾ cup firmly packed brown sugar
½ cup sugar
¼ cup cocoa powder
½ cup chopped pecans
1 cup jumbo chocolate chips
1¾ cups all-purpose flour, mixed with 1 teaspoon baking soda, 1 teaspoon baking powder, and ¼ teaspoon salt

Layer first 3 ingredients in wide-mouth canning jar. Wipe around inside of jar after cocoa powder. Continue layering ingredients; press each layer firmly in place before adding the next ingredient. Put lid on tight.

Attach these instructions: Empty jar of cookie mix into large mixing bowl. Use your hands to thoroughly blend mix. Add 1½ sticks butter, softened, 1 egg, slightly beaten, and 1 teaspoon vanilla. Mix until completely blended. The dough is sticky. You will need to finish mixing by hand. Shape into walnut-size balls. Place 2 inches apart on sprayed baking sheet. Bake at 350° for 11–13 minutes. Makes 3 dozen cookies.

Ofe Gonzales (Recipes to Remember)

White Chocolate Macadamia Nut Oatmeal Cookies

1 cup butter, softened
½ cup granulated sugar
1 cup brown sugar
2 eggs
1 teaspoon vanilla
1½ cups all-purpose flour
1 teaspoon baking soda
3 cups oatmeal
1 (1-pound) box Baker's white chocolate, chopped
1 (3½-ounce) jar macadamia nuts, chopped

Preheat oven to 350°. Cream butter and sugars together; add eggs and vanilla; blend well. Stir flour and baking soda into large bowl; blend in oatmeal. Pour in butter mixture and mix well. Scrape bottom and sides of bowl. Fold chocolate and nuts into batter. Make 1-inch dough balls and place on cookie sheets about 2 inches apart. Bake 12–15 minutes, or until golden brown. Makes about 3½ dozen cookies.

Barbara Wilson (Our Favorite Recipes)

Neiman-Marcus Cookies

2 cups butter, softened
2 cups granulated sugar
2 cups brown sugar
4 eggs
2 teaspoons vanilla
4 cups all-purpose flour
5 cups blended oatmeal*
1 teaspoon salt
2 teaspoons baking powder
2 teaspoons baking soda
2 (12-ounce) packages chocolate chips
1 (8-ounce) Hershey's bar, grated
3 cups chopped nuts

Cream butter and both sugars; add eggs and vanilla. Mix together with flour, oatmeal, salt, baking powder, and soda. Add chips, grated Hershey's bar, and nuts. Roll into balls and place 2 inches apart on cookie sheet. Bake 6 minutes at 375°. Makes about 110 cookies.

*Process oatmeal in a blender to a fine powder.

(Country Favorites)

Chocolate Pecan Cookies

2 sticks butter, softened
2 cups sugar
3 eggs
3 teaspoons vanilla
6 tablespoons cocoa
3½ cups all-purpose flour
3 teaspoons baking powder
2 pounds pecans
⅔ cup milk

Cream butter and sugar, then add eggs; add vanilla; mix well. Add cocoa, flour, baking powder, and pecans to creamed mixture; mix well. Add milk; mix well. Drop by teaspoons onto greased baking sheet; bake at 350° for 15–20 minutes. Makes about 3 dozen cookies.

Rose Whorton (Cookins for Gulf Coast Council / Blue)

Chocolate Truffle Cookies

1 cup butter, softened
¾ cup powdered sugar, divided
1½ teaspoons vanilla
1 (1-ounce) square unsweetened chocolate, melted
2¼ cups all-purpose flour
¼ teaspoon salt
½ (12-ounce) package chocolate chips
2 tablespoons cocoa

Heat oven to 375°. Lightly grease cookie sheets. In large bowl, cream butter and ½ cup powdered sugar. Blend in vanilla and chocolate. Lightly spoon flour into measuring cup; level off. At low speed, blend flour and salt into creamed mixture. By hand fold in chocolate chips. Shape into 1-inch balls; place on prepared cookie sheets. Bake at 375° for 10–12 minutes; cool.

In small bowl, combine remaining ¼ cup powdered sugar and cocoa. Roll cooled cookies in mixture. Makes 4 dozen cookies.

Doris Owens (Cookins for Gulf Coast Council / Red)

The first Picturephone test system, built in 1956, was crude—it transmitted an image only once every two seconds. By 1964 a complete experimental system, the "Mod 1," had been developed, but failed miserably. It wasn't until decades later, with improvements in speed, resolution, miniaturization, and the incorporation of Picturephone into another piece of desktop equipment, the computer, that the promise of a personal video communication system was realized.

Texas Ranger Cookies

¾ cup sugar
1 cup brown sugar
2 eggs
1 cup butter, softened
1 tablespoon vanilla
2 cups all-purpose flour
2 teaspoons baking soda
1 teaspoon baking powder
2 cups cornflakes
1 cup oatmeal
2 cups chopped pecans
1 cup shredded coconut

Preheat oven to 350°. Cream together sugars, eggs, butter, and vanilla. Sift together flour, baking soda, and baking powder; add to creamed mixture. Fold in remaining ingredients; mix very well. Form into 1-inch balls and place about 2 inches apart on cookie sheet. Bake at 350° for 12–15 minutes. Makes about 4 dozen cookies.

Barbara Wilson (Our Favorite Recipes)

My Oatmeal Cookies

2 cups brown sugar
1 cup shortening
2 eggs
1 cup flaked coconut
2 cups quick cooking oats
2 cups all-purpose flour
1 teaspoon vanilla
½ teaspoon salt
1½ teaspoons baking soda
1½ teaspoons baking powder
½ (12-ounce) package butterscotch morsels
½ cup chopped pecans

Combine ingredients well. Drop by spoonfuls onto lightly sprayed cookie sheet. Bake at 275° for 15–18 minutes.

Margie Ortiz (Recipes to Remember)

Peanut Butter Sandies

2 cups all-purpose flour
1 teaspoon baking powder
½ teaspoon baking soda
½ cup oil
½ cup smooth peanut butter
6 tablespoons butter, softened
1 cup powdered sugar, sifted
½ cup packed brown sugar
1½ teaspoons vanilla
1 large egg

Sift together flour, baking powder, and baking soda; set aside. Combine oil, peanut butter, and butter; beat till blended. Add powdered sugar and brown sugar; beat till fluffy and smooth. Beat in vanilla and egg. Add dry ingredients, mixing thoroughly. Shape dough into 1-inch balls and place on cookie sheet about 2 inches apart. Press with fingers into round cookie. Bake at 350° for 10–12 minutes, or until golden brown. Makes about 3 dozen cookies.

Barbara Wilson (Our Favorite Recipes)

Sand Tarts

½ cup butter, softened
2 tablespoons sugar
⅛ teaspoon salt
1 teaspoon vanilla
1 cup all-purpose flour
1 cup finely chopped nuts
Powdered sugar to finish

Combine all ingredients except powdered sugar. Chill; roll into quarter moon shapes. Bake on ungreased pan at 350° for 15–17 minutes. Cool 3 minutes; roll in powdered sugar; cool on rack and dust with more powdered sugar. Makes 12–15 tarts.

Edris Toney (Cookins for Gulf Coast Council / Blue)

Icebox Cookies

1 pound butter or margarine, softened
1 (1-pound) box brown sugar
2 eggs
¼ teaspoon baking soda
1 teaspoon vanilla
6 cups sifted all-purpose flour
Chopped nuts, chocolate chips, or dried fruit (optional)

Combine ingredients and mix well. May divide dough and add different optional ingredients to each half. Divide dough into 3 or 4 rolls and chill in refrigerator. Slice and bake at 350° for 10–12 minutes. Makes about 9 dozen cookies.

(Country Favorites)

Butter Cookies

¾ cup butter, softened
¾ cup sugar
2 egg yolks, beaten
2 cups cake flour (sifted before measuring)
1 teaspoon vanilla

Cream butter and sugar until light and fluffy. Add egg yolks and beat well. Add flour gradually and mix after each addition. Add vanilla; blend. Divide dough in half. Shape into rolls approximately 1¾ inches in diameter. Slice and bake on cookie sheet for 8–10 minutes at 350°.

(Country Favorites)

Potato Chip Cookies

1 cup butter, softened
½ cup sugar
¾ cup crushed ridged potato chips
½ cup ground pecans
1 teaspoon vanilla
2 cups all-purpose flour

In mixing bowl, cream butter and sugar. Stir in potato chips and pecans. Add vanilla; mix well. Stir in flour just until dough pulls away from sides of bowl and forms a ball. Shape into 1-inch balls; place 2 inches apart on greased baking sheets. Flatten with glass dipped in flour. Bake at 350° for 12–15 minutes, or until lightly browned. Makes about 5 dozen.

Karen Strickland (Recipes to Remember)

Teatime Tasties

½ (8-ounce) package cream cheese, softened
½ cup plus 1 tablespoon butter, softened, divided
1 cup all-purpose flour
1 egg
¾ cup brown sugar
1 teaspoon vanilla
⅔ cup chopped pecans

Blend cream cheese and ½ cup butter; add flour and mix well. Put in refrigerator 1 hour. Beat egg; add brown sugar, 1 tablespoon butter, vanilla, and pecans. Shape dough into small balls; press in miniature muffin pan; fill with pecan mixture. Bake at 350° until golden brown.

Brenda Greene (Cookins for Gulf Coast Council / Red)

Tea Dainties

2 eggs
1 cup light brown sugar
⅔ cup sifted all-purpose flour
¼ teaspoon baking powder
½ teaspoon salt
1½ cups chopped walnuts

Beat eggs; add brown sugar. Sift flour, baking powder, and salt together; add to egg mixture; blend thoroughly. Add walnuts. Drop from teaspoon onto greased cookie sheet ½ inch apart. Bake in moderate 350° oven 12 minutes. Makes about 2 dozen.

Yvonne Morrison (Cookins for Gulf Coast Council / Red)

Tea Cakes

¾ cup shortening
2½ cups sugar
2 eggs
2 teaspoons vanilla
1 teaspoon allspice
¼ teaspoon cinnamon
¼ teaspoon nutmeg
1 cup evaporated milk
3½ cups self-rising flour

Cream shortening and sugar. Add remaining ingredients except flour; mix thoroughly. Add flour, one cup at a time. Roll on floured board. Dough will be a little hard to work with at first, but it will get firmer as you re-roll. Cut with glass or cookie cutter. Place on ungreased cookie sheet. Bake at 350° until cookie bottoms begin to turn brown. Makes about 24 cookies.

(Country Favorites)

Pecan Pie Bars

1 (8-ounce) can refrigerated crescent dinner rolls
1 egg, beaten
½ cup chopped pecans
½ cup sugar
½ cup corn syrup
1 tablespoon butter, melted
½ teaspoon vanilla

Heat oven to 375°. Lightly grease 9x13-inch pan. Separate crescent dough into 2 large rectangles. Press rectangles over bottom and ½ inch up sides of greased pan to form crust; seal perforation. Bake crust at 375° for 5 minutes. In medium bowl, combine remaining ingredients. Pour over partially baked crust. Bake at 375° for 18–22 minutes, or until brown. Cool; cut into bars. Makes 2 dozen bars.

Donna Wilcox (Cookins for Gulf Coast Council / Red)

Pecan Puffs

1 pound butter, softened
4 teaspoons vanilla
8 tablespoons sugar
2 cups chopped pecans
4 cups all-purpose flour
Powdered sugar

Cream butter; add vanilla and sugar; mix well. Mix pecans into flour; add to creamed mixture. Shape dough into balls and bake at 325° for 15 minutes. Roll in powdered sugar while slightly warm. Makes about 4 dozen.

Rose Whorton (Cookins for Gulf Coast Council / Blue)

Rum Ball Cookies

1 (12-ounce) package vanilla wafers
1 cup chopped pecans
1 cup powdered sugar
4 tablespoons light corn syrup
½–¾ cup rum

Crush wafers and nuts, then add sugar and syrup; mix well. Gradually stir in liquor until mixture holds together. Form into balls and roll in additional powdered sugar or, for variety, roll in flaked coconut.

Margie Ortiz (Recipes to Remember)

Is It Cheese?

1 stick butter
1 (18¼-ounce) package yellow or white cake mix
⅓ cup plus ¼ cup toasted coconut, divided
1 (21-ounce) can cherry pie filling
1 pint sour cream
2 egg yolks
2 teaspoons vanilla
4 teaspoons sugar
1 tablespoon cinnamon

Melt butter in medium saucepan; stir in cake mix. Remove from heat and gently press into 9x13-inch baking pan. Sprinkle with ⅓ cup coconut. Pour pie filling over and spread to edges. Mix sour cream, egg yolks, and vanilla together. Spread over top of pie filling. Combine sugar, cinnamon, and remaining ¼ cup coconut; sprinkle over top of cream mixture. Bake at 350° for 25–30 minutes. When cool, cut in squares. Makes 15–18 squares.

Geraldine Kyker (Cookins for Gulf Coast Council / Blue)

Peanut Patties

3 cups sugar
½ cup water
1 cup light Karo syrup
3 cups raw peanuts
1 stick margarine
1 tablespoon vanilla
Dash of salt
3–4 drops red food coloring

Combine sugar, water, Karo, and peanuts in heavy 3-quart saucepan. On medium-high, bring to a boil, stirring constantly for 5 minutes. (When it begins to boil in the middle, start timing.) Remove from heat; add margarine, vanilla, salt, and coloring; cool slightly. Beat by hand until creamy and unglossy. Drop by teaspoonfuls onto ungreased foil, which has been laid over newspaper for heat protection.

(Country Favorites)

Buckeyes

2 sticks butter, softened
1 (16-ounce) jar peanut butter
1 (1-pound) box powdered sugar
6 ounces chocolate chips
⅓ bar paraffin

Whip butter till soft; blend in peanut butter. Add sugar and blend well. Chill dough until it becomes easy to handle, then roll into balls and chill thoroughly. Put toothpicks in center of each ball. Melt chocolate chips and paraffin in top of double boiler; blend well. Dip each ball into mixture, leaving a portion uncoated to form eye. Place on wax paper to set. Keep refrigerated. Makes 75–100 buckeyes.

Debra Martin (Our Favorite Recipes)

Millionaires Candy

1 (14-ounce) package caramels, peeled
2 tablespoons water
2–3 cups pecan halves
1 large Hershey's bar or 10 small ones
¼ cup paraffin wax

Melt caramels with water. Add pecans and drop by spoonfuls onto wax paper. Melt chocolate in double boiler; add melted paraffin. Dip caramel-pecan drops in chocolate and paraffin mixture. Set on wax paper to dry.

(Country Favorites)

Date-Nut Roll Candy

2 cups sugar
1 cup milk
2 tablespoons butter
1½ cups chopped dates
1 cup chopped nuts
1 teaspoon vanilla

In saucepan, combine sugar, milk, butter, and dates; cook to 240° or soft-ball stage. Remove from heat; cool; beat. Add nuts and vanilla. Pour onto damp cloth and roll.

Ouida Alexander (Cookins for Gulf Coast Council / Red)

Festive Holiday Bark

1 (16-ounce) package vanilla-flavored candy coating, chopped
2 cups small pretzel twists
½ cup red and green candy-coated chocolate pieces

Line cookie sheet with wax paper. Melt candy coating in medium saucepan over low heat, stirring constantly. Add remaining ingredients; toss to coat. Spread mixture thinly on wax paper-lined cookie sheet. Let stand until set. Break into pieces. Makes about 42 pieces.

(Recipes to Remember)

Peanut Butter Fudge

2 cups sugar
1 cup evaporated milk
3 tablespoons butter
1 cup miniature marshmallows
1 cup chunky peanut butter
1 teaspoon vanilla

Heat electric skillet to 280°. In skillet, combine first 3 ingredients. Boil 5 minutes, stirring constantly. Turn off heat; add marshmallows, peanut butter, and vanilla; blend well. Pour into greased 8-inch square pan. Cool and cut into squares. Makes about 2 pounds candy.

Linda O'Dell (Our Favorite Recipes)

White Christmas Fudge

2¼ cups sugar
½ cup sour cream
¼ cup milk
1 tablespoon light corn syrup
2 tablespoons margarine
¼ teaspoon salt
2 teaspoons vanilla
1 cup chopped pecans
1⅓ cups cut-up candied red cherries

Combine sugar, sour cream, milk, corn syrup, margarine, and salt in heavy saucepan. Stir on medium heat until sugar is dissolved and mixture reaches a boil. Cook to 238° on candy thermometer. Remove from heat and allow to stand until mixture begins to lose gloss and hold shape. Quickly stir in pecans and cherries. Turn into oiled 8x8-inch pan. Let stand till firm. Cut into squares.

Kay Bauch (Cookins for Gulf Coast Council / Red)

Palomino Fudge

2 cups sugar
1 cup whole milk
½ teaspoon salt
1 teaspoon margarine or butter
1 teaspoon vanilla
½ cup marshmallow crème
½ cup chopped maraschino cherries

Butter sides of 2-quart saucepan. Combine sugar, milk, and salt. Heat and stir over medium heat until sugar dissolves and mixture comes to a boil. Cook to soft-ball stage, stirring only as necessary. Remove from heat; add margarine and cool to 110°, without stirring. Add vanilla, beating vigorously until candy begins to hold shape. Add marshmallow crème; beat until very thick and beginning to lose gloss. Quickly stir in cherries and spread in buttered shallow pan or dish. Score in squares while warm; cut when firm. Makes about 24 pieces.

Variation: For Maple-Pecan Fudge: Omit cherries; add 1 teaspoon maple flavoring; decorate each square with pecan half.

(Country Favorites)

Poncho Roberts' Peanut Brittle

2 cups sugar
1 cup Karo syrup
2 tablespoons butter
½ cup water
1 (12.5-ounce) can red-skin Spanish peanuts
2 teaspoons baking soda
2 teaspoons vanilla

Combine sugar, syrup, butter, and water; cook to soft-ball stage (10–12 minutes). Add peanuts and cook till syrup is as brown as the peanut husks (7–9 minutes). Remove from heat; add soda and vanilla. Mix quickly and thoroughly, then pour onto buttered foil. Cool about an hour before breaking into pieces.

Poncho Roberts (Our Favorite Recipes)

Texas Pecan Brittle

2 cups sugar
1 cup light corn syrup
½ cup water
½ teaspoon salt
3 cups pecans
2 tablespoons baking soda
2 tablespoons butter
1 teaspoon vanilla

Combine sugar, corn syrup, water, and salt in large heavy saucepan; boil together until mixture spins a thread off when lifted (240°). Add pecans and cook until mixture turns light brown, stirring. Add baking soda, butter, and vanilla; stir and pour onto buttered cookie sheet. Let run thin, break up, and serve.

Leann Hall (Cookins for Gulf Coast Council / Blue)

Almond Toffee Candy

2 sticks margarine
1 cup sliced almonds
1 cup sugar
1 tablespoon ice water
1 (16-ounce) bottle white Karo
1 (6-ounce) Hershey's chocolate bar

Put everything except chocolate into saucepan; cook on medium heat. Stir constantly about 20 minutes, or until candy turns light brown (like light brown sugar); turn out onto ungreased cookie sheet. Place chocolate on top and spread as it melts. Cool at room temperature and then put in refrigerator till chilled. Break up with knife.

Margie Case (Cookins for Gulf Coast Council / Red)

English Toffee

1 cup blanched, slivered almonds, toasted
1 cup butter or margarine
1 cup sugar
⅓ cup semisweet chocolate bits

Chop almonds and spread ½ cup in bottom of buttered 7x11-inch pan. Combine butter and sugar in heavy skillet; cook, stirring, until boiling point is reached. Boil over medium heat, stirring constantly to soft-crack stage (270°–280°). Pour carefully over almonds. Let stand about 10 minutes, until top is set. Sprinkle chocolate over top of candy. When heat of candy has melted chocolate, smooth with spatula. Sprinkle remaining almonds over chocolate. Let stand until cold; break into squares. Makes about 1½ pounds.

(Country Favorites)

Western Pralines

2 cups sugar
1 teaspoon baking soda
1 cup buttermilk
⅛ teaspoon salt
2 tablespoons butter
2½ cups pecan halves

In 3½-quart heavy saucepan, combine sugar, soda, buttermilk, and salt. Cook over high heat about 5 minutes (or 210° on candy thermometer); stir often and scrape bottom of pan. Mixture will foam up! Add butter and pecans. Over medium heat, continue cooking, stirring constantly and scraping bottom and sides of pan, until candy reaches soft-ball stage (234°). Remove from heat and cool slightly, only about 2 minutes. Beat with spoon until thick and creamy. Drop from tablespoon onto sheet of aluminum foil or wax paper; let cool. Makes about 20 pralines, 2 inches in diameter.

(Country Favorites)

Pies and Other Desserts

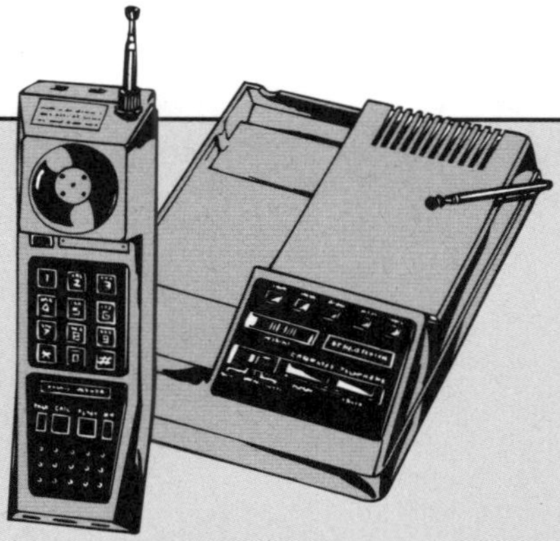

1980
Cordless

Cordless phones first appeared around 1980 and were primitive by today's standards. These phones, without cables or cords, chiefly used radio frequency and were initially given a frequency of 27 MHz by the Federal Communications Commission (FCC), which is the same frequency range used by CB radio. The base needs a separate power source to transmit the signal to the handset. The cordless handset is powered by a battery that is recharged by the base station. By 1998 Caller ID was introduced, 2.4 GHz frequencies opened, and a Digital Spread Spectrum signal became available. This added security and spread the signal 360 degrees from the base to the handset, so there were no dead spots and distance could go to a quarter mile. As additional features were added, prices dropped and demand rose. Consumers now wanted all their phones to be cordless. This created a new set of problems. If there was ever a power failure, you wouldn't have any working phones.

Buttermilk Pie

1½ cups sugar
2 rounded tablespoons cornstarch
¾ stick margarine
3 eggs
½ cup buttermilk
1 teaspoon lemon extract
Few drops almond extract
⅛ teaspoon salt
1 (8-inch) pie crust

Cream together sugar, cornstarch, margarine, and eggs. Add buttermilk, lemon extract, almond extract, and salt. Pour into pie shell; bake 10 minutes at 400°. Turn down to 350° and bake until golden brown, about 20 minutes.

(Country Favorites)

Buttermilk Pecan Pie

½ cup butter, softened
2 cups sugar
2 teaspoons vanilla
3 eggs
3 tablespoons all-purpose flour
¼ teaspoon salt
1 cup buttermilk
½ cup chopped pecans
1 (9-inch) pie shell

Preheat oven to 300°. Cream butter and sugar until light and fluffy, adding ½ cup sugar at a time. Blend in vanilla. Add eggs, one at a time. Combine flour and salt; add small amount at a time. Add buttermilk. Sprinkle pecans in bottom of pie crust; pour custard mixture over pecans and bake 1 hour 30 minutes at 300°. The top browns as it cooks. Best served at room temperature.

Tina M. Salinas (Cookins for Gulf Coast Council / Red)

Miracle Pie

- 1 cup sugar
- ¼ cup butter, softened
- 4 eggs
- ½ cup all-purpose flour
- 2 cups milk
- 1 cup flaked coconut
- ¼ teaspoon salt
- ½ teaspoon baking powder
- 1 teaspoon vanilla

Blend all ingredients in blender. Pour into sprayed 10-inch pie plate. Bake 1 hour at 350°. A crust will form on the bottom, filling in the middle, and the coconut will rise to the top. It's a miracle.

Belinda Estrada (Recipes to Remember)

5-Minute Creamy Coconut Pie

- 1 (3-ounce) package cream cheese, softened
- 1 tablespoon sugar
- ½ cup milk
- 1⅓ cups flaked coconut
- 1 (8-ounce) container Cool Whip, thawed
- ½ teaspoon almond extract (optional)
- 1 (9-inch) graham cracker crust

Combine cream cheese, sugar, milk, and coconut in blender container. Cover and blend at LOW speed 30 seconds. Fold in whipped topping and extract. Spoon into pie crust; freeze until firm, about 4 hours. Let stand at room temperature about 15 minutes or longer before cutting. Store leftover pie in freezer. Serves 6–8.

Leann Hall (Cookins for Gulf Coast Council / Blue)

Coconut Cream Pie

3 egg yolks
2½ cups milk
1½ cups sugar
7 tablespoons all-purpose flour
1 cup flaked coconut
1 teaspoon vanilla
1 (9-inch) pie crust, baked

In saucepan, beat eggs; add milk. Gradually add mixture of sugar and flour. Cook until thick, stirring constantly. Add coconut and vanilla; pour into baked pie crust.

MERINGUE:
3 egg whites
½ teaspoon vanilla
¼ teaspoon cream of tartar
⅓ cup sugar
Flaked coconut for garnish

In mixer bowl, beat egg whites, vanilla, and cream of tartar till soft peaks form. Gradually add sugar, beating till stiff peaks form. Put on pie, pushing to edge of crust to seal. Sprinkle coconut on top and brown.

Doris Owens (Cookins for Gulf Coast Council / Red)

In 1978, American Telephone and Telegraph's (AT&T) Bell Laboratories began testing a mobile telephone system based on hexagonal geographical regions called cells. As the caller's vehicle passed from one cell to another, an automatic switching system would transfer the telephone call to another cell without interruption. The cellular telephone system began nationwide usage in the United States in 1983.

Pear Pie with Ginger Topping

1 cup all-purpose flour
½ cup firmly packed brown sugar
½ cup margarine, softened
½ teaspoon ginger, divided
½ cup chopped nuts
3 tablespoons cornstarch
⅛ teaspoon salt
2 tablespoons margarine, melted
½ cup dark corn syrup
½ teaspoon grated lemon rind
1 teaspoon lemon juice
4 medium-size fresh pears, cored, peeled, thinly sliced
1 (9-inch) pastry shell, unbaked

In bowl, mix together flour, brown sugar, ½ cup margarine, and ¼ teaspoon ginger until coarse crumbs form. Stir in nuts; set aside. In large bowl, stir together cornstarch, salt, and remaining ginger. Stir in 2 tablespoons melted margarine, corn syrup, lemon rind, and juice until smooth. Add pears, tossing until well coated with corn syrup mixture; spoon into pastry shell. Sprinkle topping over unbaked pie. Bake a in 400° oven 15 minutes; reduce heat to 350°, and continue baking 30 minutes, or until topping and crust are browned; cool. Top with vanilla or coffee ice cream, if desired. Serves 6–8.

Robbie Daw (Cookins for Gulf Coast Council / Blue)

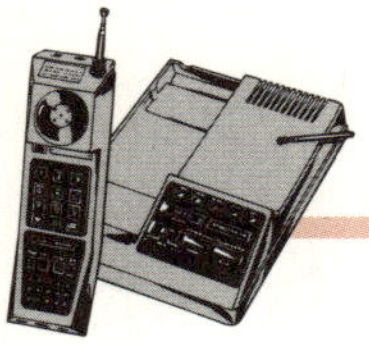

Strawberry Glamour Pie

1 (9-inch) deep-dish pie crust, or 2 small ones
2 egg whites, room temperature
½ teaspoon vinegar
¼ teaspoon salt
⅓ cup plus ¾ cup sugar, divided
1½–2 cups sliced fresh strawberries, divided
3 tablespoons cornstarch
½ cup water
Red food coloring
Cool Whip
Strawberry halves for garnish

Preheat oven to 350° (or 325° for glass pans). Prick crust with fork and bake until light brown; cool. Beat egg whites with vinegar and salt to soft peaks. Add ⅓ cup sugar, beating to stiff peaks. Spread on bottom and sides of baked crust. Place in 375° oven until light brown; cool.

Mash strawberries with ¾ cup sugar. Combine in saucepan with cornstarch and water; cook until thick. Tint with food coloring; cool. Spread filling over meringue. Top with Cool Whip and garnish with strawberry halves. Serves 6–8.

Jan Wyman (Cookins for Gulf Coast Council / Blue)

Mom's Pineapple Pie

1½ cups sugar
2 tablespoons butter, melted
2 tablespoons all-purpose flour
3 eggs
1 can flaked coconut (optional)
1 (20-ounce) can crushed pineapple, drained
1 teaspoon vanilla
1 (9-inch) pie crust

Combine ingredients. Bake in pie crust at 350° for 50–60 minutes till firm.

Linda Rape (Cookins for Gulf Coast Council / Red)

Pineapple Sour Cream Pie

1 cup sugar, divided
¼ cup all-purpose flour
½ teaspoon salt
1 (20-ounce) can crushed pineapple, drained
1 cup sour cream
1 tablespoon lemon juice
2 egg yolks, slightly beaten
1 (9-inch) pie shell, baked
2 egg whites
¼ teaspoon cream of tartar
½ teaspoon vanilla

In saucepan, combine ¾ cup sugar, flour, and salt; stir in next 3 ingredients; cook and stir till mixture thickens and comes to a boil; cook 2 minutes. Stir small amount of hot mixture into egg yolks, return to hot mixture, stirring constantly. Cook and stir 2 minutes; cook to room temperature. Spoon into pie shell. Beat egg whites, cream of tartar, and vanilla to soft peaks. Gradually add remaining ¼ cup sugar, beating till stiff and glossy; top pie with mixture. Bake at 350° for 12–15 minutes.

(Cookins for Gulf Coast Council / Blue)

Creamy Lemon Meringue Pie

3 eggs, separated
1 (14-ounce) can condensed milk
½ cup lemon juice
1 teaspoon grated lemon rind
1 butter-flavored Ready Crust pie crust
¼ teaspoon cream of tartar
⅓ cup sugar

Preheat oven to 350°. In medium bowl, beat egg yolks; stir in condensed milk, lemon juice, and rind; turn into pie crust. In small mixer bowl, beat egg whites (at room temperature) with cream of tartar until foamy; gradually add sugar, beating until stiff but not dry. Spread meringue on top of filling, sealing carefully to edge of crust. Place filled pie on cookie sheet in oven and bake 12–15 minutes, or until meringue is golden brown. Cool; chill. Serves 6–8.

Leann Hall (Cookins for Gulf Coast Council / Blue)

Impossible Piña Colada Pie

4 eggs
¼ cup milk
¼ cup rum, or 2 teaspoons rum extract plus 2 tablespoons milk
2 tablespoons butter, softened
1 (15-ounce) can cream of coconut
1 (8-ounce) can crushed pineapple, well drained
½ cup buttermilk baking mix
1 cup flaked coconut

Heat oven to 350°. Grease a 10-inch pie plate. Beat eggs, milk, rum, butter, cream of coconut, crushed pineapple, and baking mix until well blended, 30 seconds in blender on high or 1 minute with hand beater. Pour into plate. Sprinkle with coconut. Bake until knife inserted in center comes out clean, 40–45 minutes.

Lois Parker (Cookins for Gulf Coast Council / Red)

Macadamia Key Lime Pie

CRUST:

½ (15-ounce) package refrigerated pie crust, room temperature

½ cup plus 1 tablespoon macadamia nuts, coarsely chopped

Preheat oven to 450°. Gently unfold pie crust onto lightly floured surface. Roll to 12-inch circle. Place crust in a deep-dish pie plate, pressing dough into bottom and up sides. Prick bottom and sides using pastry tool. Sprinkle ½ cup nuts over bottom. Bake 10–11 minutes, or until crust is golden brown; cool completely.

FILLING:

4 large limes

1 (8-ounce) package cream cheese, softened

1 (14-ounce) can condensed milk

3–4 drops each: green and yellow food coloring

1 (12-ounce) carton whipped topping, thawed

Additional lime slices for garnish

Zest limes to measure 3 teaspoons zest. Juice limes to measure ½ cup lime juice. Combine cream cheese and condensed milk in bowl; whisk until smooth. Stir zest, juice, and food coloring into cream cheese mixture; mix well. Fold in 2 cups whipped topping. Pour mixture into crust. Refrigerate at least 30 minutes.

In small sauté pan, toast remaining 1 tablespoon nuts over medium heat until light golden brown, stirring constantly. Garnish top of pie with remaining whipped topping and lime slices. Sprinkle with nuts.

Cathi Garza (Recipes to Remember)

Fluffy Peanut Butter Pie

CHOCOLATE CRUNCH CRUST:

½ cup butter
½ (12-ounce) package semi-sweet chocolate morsels
3 cups oven-toasted rice cereal

In medium saucepan, melt butter and chocolate morsels over low heat. Remove from heat; gently stir in cereal. Stir until cereal is coated with chocolate. Press in bottom and up sides of lightly greased 9-inch pie plate. Chill 2–3 hours. Fill with desired pie filling.

PEANUT BUTTER PIE:

1 (8-ounce) package cream cheese, softened
1 (14-ounce) can condensed milk
¾–1 cup creamy peanut butter
3 tablespoons reconstituted lemon juice
1 teaspoon vanilla
1 cup whipping cream, whipped
1–2 teaspoons chocolate-flavored syrup

In large bowl, beat cheese until fluffy; add condensed milk and peanut butter, beating until smooth. Stir in lemon juice and vanilla. Fold in whipped cream. Turn into prepared pie crust. Drizzle syrup over top of pie; gently marble with knife. Chill 4 hours or until set. Refrigerate leftovers.

Marty Horn (Cookins for Gulf Coast Council / Red)

Festive Pumpkin Pie

SPICED NUT CRUST:

½ cup butter or margarine
1 cup unsifted all-purpose flour
½ cup finely chopped pecans or walnuts
¼ cup firmly packed light brown sugar
½ teaspoon ground cinnamon
10–12 pecans or walnut halves (optional)

In small saucepan, melt butter; remove from heat. Add flour, nuts, brown sugar, and cinnamon; mix well. Pat on bottom and sides of 9-inch pie plate. If desired, press nut halves onto rim of crust. Fill with desired filling; bake as directed.

FESTIVE PUMPKIN PIE:

1 (16-ounce) can pumpkin
1 (14-ounce) can condensed milk
2 eggs
1 teaspoon ground cinnamon
½ teaspoon ground ginger
½ teaspoon ground nutmeg
½ teaspoon salt
Whipped cream (optional)

Preheat oven to 350°. In large bowl, combine pumpkin, condensed milk, eggs, cinnamon, ginger, nutmeg, and salt; mix well. Turn into prepared crust; bake 35–40 minutes, or until knife inserted 1 inch from edge comes out clean. Cool before serving. If desired, garnish with whipped cream. Refrigerate leftovers.

Marty Horn (Cookins for Gulf Coast Council / Red)

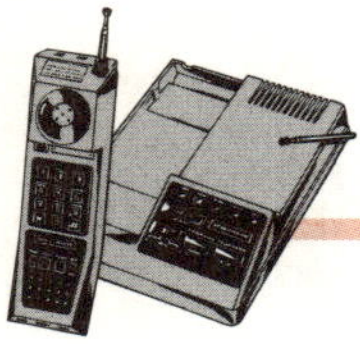

Sweet Potato Pie

1 (29-ounce) can sweet potatoes, drained
1 stick butter, softened
1 cup sugar
½ teaspoon ground ginger
¼ teaspoon ground cloves
1¼ teaspoons ground cinnamon
½ teaspoon ground nutmeg
2 eggs, beaten
1 cup milk
1 (9-inch) pie shell, unbaked

Mash potatoes in large bowl. Cream butter and sugar; add ginger, cloves, cinnamon, and nutmeg; blend in with sweet potatoes. Add eggs and milk to mixture, mixing till well blended. Pour into pie shell; bake in preheated 350° oven about 60 minutes. When it browns and begins to leave sides of crust, it is ready. Check center with knife.

Catherine Losack (Cookins for Gulf Coast Council / Red)

Pecan Pie

¾ cup sugar
2 tablespoons all-purpose flour
1 teaspoon salt
½ cup light corn syrup
½ cup dark corn syrup
2 eggs, one at a time
½ cup evaporated milk
1 cup chopped pecans
1 teaspoon vanilla
1 (9-inch) pastry crust

Mix first 3 ingredients in a 1½-quart bowl. Stir in rest of ingredients except crust. Pour mixture into crust. Bake in 375° oven for 50 minutes, or until firm. Cool before serving.

Billy Cash (Our Favorite Recipes)

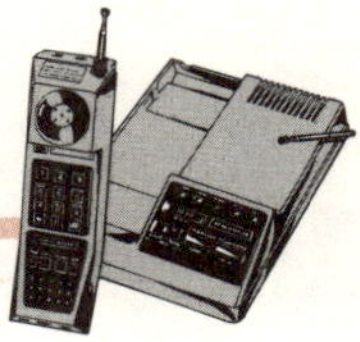

Small Pecan Tarts

CRUST:

1 cup all-purpose flour
½ cup margarine
1 (3-ounce) package cream cheese, softened

Blend ingredients; press into small muffin pans.

FILLING:

1 egg
½ cup light brown sugar
6 teaspoons chopped pecans
Dash of salt
½ teaspoon vanilla
1 teaspoon margarine

Combine all ingredients. Spoon Filling into Crust. Bake at 350° until brown.

Linda O'Dell (Our Favorite Recipes)

Cheesecake Pie

1⅓ cups fine graham cracker crumbs
¼ cup butter, melted
3 (3-ounce) packages cream cheese, softened
½ cup plus 5 tablespoons sugar, divided
2 eggs, beaten
1 teaspoon vanilla, divided
2 cups sour cream
⅛ teaspoon cinnamon

Mix graham cracker crumbs and butter and press into bottom and sides of 9-inch pie pan. Bake 5 minutes at 350°. Reduce oven to 325°. Mix cream cheese and ½ cup sugar well. Add beaten eggs and ½ teaspoon vanilla. Pour into crust and bake 20 minutes, or until firm.

In bowl, mix sour cream, remaining ½ teaspoon vanilla, 5 tablespoons sugar, and cinnamon; spread on pie and return to oven; bake 5 minutes. Cool, then chill.

Mary Jordan (Cookins for Gulf Coast Council / Blue)

Dutch Brownie Pie

(With Cinnamon Hot Fudge Sauce)

4 ounces sweet cooking chocolate
5 tablespoons butter, softened, divided
1 (3-ounce) package cream cheese, softened
1 cup sugar, divided
3 eggs, divided
1 tablespoon plus ½ cup all-purpose flour, divided
¼ teaspoon cherry extract
½ teaspoon baking powder
¼ teaspoon salt
1 teaspoon vanilla extract
½ teaspoon almond extract
½ cup slivered almonds
Vanilla ice cream
Cinnamon Hot Fudge Sauce

In saucepan, melt chocolate and 3 tablespoons butter over very low heat, stirring constantly; cool. In small mixer bowl, blend remaining 2 tablespoons butter with cream cheese until fluffy. Gradually add ¼ cup sugar, beating well. Blend in 1 egg, 1 tablespoon flour, and cherry extract; set aside.

In large mixer bowl, beat remaining 2 eggs until foamy. Gradually add remaining ¾ cup sugar, beating until thickened. Blend in remaining ½ cup flour, baking powder, and salt. Stir in chocolate mixture, vanilla and almond extracts, and nuts. Spread half the chocolate batter evenly in greased 11-inch pie plate. Spread cream cheese mixture over top. Top with spoonfuls of remaining chocolate batter. Swirl top of batter lightly with a fork.

Bake at 350° for 40–50 minutes, or until top springs back when lightly pressed in center. Cool on wire rack. To serve, cut into wedges, and top with ice cream and Cinnamon Hot Fudge Sauce. Makes 10 servings.

(continued)

CINNAMON HOT FUDGE SAUCE:

1 stick butter
½ cup evaporated milk
2 cups sifted powdered sugar
½ cup chocolate-flavored dessert mix
2 teaspoons cinnamon
1 teaspoon vanilla extract

In saucepan, melt butter; add evaporated milk. Combine powdered sugar, chocolate dessert mix, and cinnamon; add to milk mixture. Cook and stir over low heat 5–10 minutes, or until of desired thickness. Remove from heat; stir in vanilla. Serve warm over pie.

Verna Dvorak (Cookins for Gulf Coast Council / Red)

Chocolate Chess Pie

1½ cups sugar
3 tablespoons cocoa
¼ cup margarine, melted
2 eggs, beaten
⅛ teaspoon salt
1 (5-ounce) can evaporated milk
1 teaspoon vanilla
½–¾ cup chopped pecans (optional)
1 (9-inch) pie shell, unbaked

Mix sugar, cocoa, and margarine; stir well. Add eggs and beat with electric mixer 2½ minutes. Add salt, milk, and vanilla; stir in pecans, if desired. Pour filling into pie shell; bake at 350° for 35–45 minutes. Serves 6–8.

Ida Lee Barron (Cookins for Gulf Coast Council / Blue)

Peach and Blueberry Cobbler

1 cup all-purpose flour
1 cup sugar, divided
1 teaspoon baking powder
½ teaspoon salt
1 egg
2 cups blueberries
3 cups sliced peaches
¼ cup butter, melted
2 tablespoons sugar mixed with ½ teaspoon cinnamon

Combine flour, ¾ cup sugar, baking powder, and salt in bowl. Stir in unbeaten egg. Mix with fork till mixture is crumbly.

Place fruit in 2-quart buttered dish. Sprinkle with remaining ¼ cup sugar and crumb mixture. Drizzle melted butter over top, then sprinkle with cinnamon sugar mixture. Bake at 375° for 35–45 minutes. Serves 8–10.

Louise Kosub (Our Favorite Recipes)

Apple Kuchen

½ cup margarine, softened
1 (18¼-ounce) package yellow cake mix
½ cup flaked coconut
1 (20-ounce) can sliced pie apples, well drained
½ cup sugar
1 teaspoon cinnamon
1 cup sour cream
2 egg yolks, or 1 whole egg

Preheat oven to 350°. Mix butter into cake mix until crumbly; mix in coconut. Pat into oblong baking pan; bake for 10 minutes. Arrange apple slices on crust. Mix sugar and cinnamon; sprinkle on apples. Blend sour cream and egg yolks. Drizzle over apples; bake 25 minutes, or until light brown.

Lela McMakin (Cookins for Gulf Coast Council / Red)

Apple Squares

1¾ cups chopped, unpeeled apples
1 cup plus 2 tablespoons sugar, divided
1½ cups all-purpose flour
½ teaspoon baking soda
1 teaspoon cinnamon
½ teaspoon nutmeg
½ teaspoon allspice
½ teaspoon salt
½ cup oil
1 egg
1 cup raisins
½ cup chopped walnuts

Combine apples and 1 cup sugar; let stand 10 minutes. Grease 8-inch cake pan and dust with sugar. Combine flour, soda, cinnamon, nutmeg, allspice, salt, oil, egg, raisins, and walnuts. Add apples and mix well. Pour batter into prepared pan and sprinkle with remaining 2 tablespoons sugar. Bake at 375° for 40 minutes. Cool in pan and cut into squares or wedges.

Note: May serve with homemade whipped cream with a little vanilla or cinnamon in it. Yum!

Dorothy Walsh (Our Favorite Recipes)

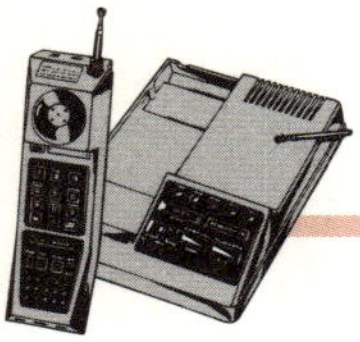

Between the Sheets

CRUST:

1 stick butter, melted
1 cup all-purpose flour
1 cup chopped pecans

Combine ingredients and spread in 9x13-inch pan just to cover bottom. Bake at 350° for 20 minutes; cool.

FILLING:

1 (8-ounce) package cream cheese, softened
1 cup powdered sugar
¾ (12-ounce) carton Cool Whip, divided

Mix ingredients together, reserving ¼ cup Cool Whip, and spread over cool Crust.

LAST LAYER:

1 (6-ounce) box chocolate instant pudding

Make according to box instructions. Spread over Filling; top with remaining Cool Whip and refrigerate at least an hour.

Michelle Stuyvesant (Recipes to Remember)

Twinkie Strawberry Dessert

20–24 Twinkies
1 (6-ounce) package strawberry Jell-O
1 (6-ounce) package vanilla instant pudding
1 (21-ounce) can strawberry pie filling
1 (16-ounce) carton Cool Whip
¼ cup chopped pecans

Layer Twinkies in 9x13-inch pan. Make Jell-O according to package directions and pour over Twinkies. Make pudding according to package directions; pour over Jell-O. Pour strawberry pie filling over pudding. Top with Cool Whip. Refrigerate overnight to set. Serves 15.

Ofe Gonzales (Our Favorite Recipes)

Dreamsicle Pudding

1 cup boiling water
1 (3-ounce) package sugar-free orange Jell-O
1 (11-ounce) can Mandarin oranges, drained, reserve juice
1 (3-ounce) package sugar-free vanilla pudding
1 (8-ounce) carton fat-free Cool Whip

Add boiling water to Jell-O and dissolve. Add juice from oranges and enough water and ice cubes to make 1 cup. Mix until ice cubes dissolve. Let set until well cooled. Add pudding mix and mix with wire whisk or mixer on low. Add Cool Whip; stir well and add oranges. Chill 2 hours, or until set.

Betty Hatcher (Our Favorite Recipes)

Bread Pudding with Rum Sauce

6 slices day-old French bread
1 teaspoon cinnamon
½ cup seedless raisins
2 tablespoons butter, melted
4 eggs
2 cups milk
1 teaspoon vanilla
2 tablespoons plus ½ cup sugar

Break bread in small pieces in 1½-quart baking dish. Sprinkle cinnamon over bread; add raisins and melted butter; toast lightly in 350° oven. Mix eggs, milk, vanilla, and sugar; pour over bread. Bake about 45 minutes. Serves 8.

RUM SAUCE:
2 cups milk
½ stick butter
½ cup sugar
2 tablespoons flour
1 tablespoon oil
1 tablespoon vanilla
Rum to taste
1 tablespoon nutmeg

Place milk, butter, and sugar in saucepan. Let come to a boil. Mix flour and oil and add to mixture to thicken. Remove from heat; stir in vanilla, rum, and nutmeg. Serve over pudding.

Robbie Daw (Cookins for Gulf Coast Council / Blue)

Jo Beth's Homemade Vanilla Ice Cream

2 (14-ounce) cans condensed milk
2 (12-ounce) cans evaporated milk
1½ cups sugar (or more)
1 teaspoon vanilla
Whole milk

Combine all ingredients except whole milk; pour into freezer container; mix well. Finish filling container to the line with whole milk. Freeze as usual.

Note: To make ice cream freeze firm, use more rock salt than usual.

(Country Favorites)

Peanut Butter Ripple Ice Cream

½ cup crunchy peanut butter
¾ cup honey
1 teaspoon orange extract
½ teaspoon ground nutmeg
2 quarts vanilla ice cream

Combine peanut butter, honey, extract, and nutmeg. Layer ice cream and peanut butter mixture into metal bowl or other 2-quart freezer container, beginning and ending with ice cream. Freeze until firm. Scoop or spoon into serving dishes. Makes 2 quarts.

(Country Favorites)

Butter Pecan Ice Cream

2 eggs, slightly beaten
1 cup sugar
½ cup packed light brown sugar
2 cups half-and-half
¼ teaspoon salt
2 cups scalded milk, cooled
1½ teaspoons vanilla extract
2 tablespoons butter
1 cup finely chopped pecans

In heavy saucepan or top of double boiler, combine eggs, sugars, cream, and salt. Cook over low heat, stirring constantly, until mixture coats a spoon; cool. Add milk and vanilla. Refrigerate several hours.

In skillet, melt butter; add pecans and sauté on medium heat, stirring constantly, being careful not to burn; cool. Pour egg mixture into cylinder of an ice cream freezer; add pecans, stirring slightly to distribute. Freeze according to manufacturer's directions. When frozen, pack ice cream in airtight containers and store in freezer. Makes 2 quarts.

(Country Favorites)

Chocolate Ice Cream

2 (12-ounce) cans evaporated milk
2 cans water
5 eggs
2 teaspoons flour
2 cups sugar
5 tablespoons cocoa
1 teaspoon vanilla
¼ teaspoon salt

Cook milk, water, eggs, flour, and sugar 20 minutes; stir. Add cocoa, vanilla, and salt. Freeze in ice cream freezer.

Susan Cordes (Cookins for Gulf Coast Council / Blue)

Fudge Sundae Sauce

1 (12-ounce) package semisweet chocolate chips
2 (1-ounce) squares unsweetened chocolate
1 cup whipping cream
¼ cup cold coffee
Dash of salt
1 teaspoon vanilla

In medium saucepan, combine chocolate, cream, coffee, and salt. Heat on low, stirring constantly, until chocolate is melted. Remove from heat; stir in vanilla. Cover and refrigerate. Reheat to serve over your favorite ice cream. Makes 2½ cups.

(Country Favorites)

Chocolate Marshmallow Sauce

2 cups sugar
1 cup boiling water
¼ cup Hershey's Cocoa
1 teaspoon vanilla
½ cup shredded fresh marshmallows, or ½ cup miniature marshmallows

Cook sugar and water in saucepan to 220°. Remove from heat; stir in cocoa, vanilla, and marshmallows until melted. Cool without stirring until bottom of pan just feels warm to hand. Beat to thicken; serve warm over ice cream. Makes 2 cups.

(Country Favorites)

Lemon Sauce

This is good served warm on bread pudding.

½ cup sugar
2 tablespoons cornstarch
1 cup water
1 egg
1 tablespoon lemon juice
1 teaspoon grated lemon peel
2 tablespoons margarine

In double boiler, mix sugar and cornstarch; add water and egg; cook till beginning to thicken. Add lemon juice, grated lemon peel, and margarine. Makes 1½ cups.

(Country Favorites)

Equivalents, Substitutions, Etc.

EQUIVALENTS:

Apple: 1 medium = 1 cup chopped

Banana: 1 medium = ⅓ cup

Berries: 1 pint = 1¾ cups

Bread: 1 slice = ½ cup soft crumbs = ¼ cup fine, dry crumbs

Broth, beef or chicken: 1 cup = 1 bouillon cube dissolved in 1 cup boiling water

Butter: 1 stick = ¼ pound = ½ cup

Cabbage: 2 pounds = 9 cups shredded or 5 cups cooked

Cheese, grated: 1 pound = 4 cups; 8 ounces = 2 cups

Chicken: 1 large boned breast = 2 cups cooked meat

Chocolate, bitter: 1 square or 1 ounce = 2 tablespoons grated

Coconut: 3½-ounce can = 1⅓ cups

Cool Whip: 8 ounces = 3 cups

Cornmeal: 1 pound = 3 cups

Crabmeat, fresh: 1 pound = 3 cups

Crackers, graham: 15 = 1 cup crushed

Crackers, saltine: 23 = 1 cup crushed

Cream, heavy: 1 cup = 2–2½ cups whipped

Cream cheese: 3 ounces = 6⅔ tablespoons

Egg whites: 8–10 = 1 cup

Eggs: 4–5 = 1 cup

Evaporated milk: 5⅓-ounce can = ⅔ cup; 12-ounce can = 1¼ cups

Flour: 1 pound = 4½ cups

Flour, self-rising: 1 cup = 1 cup all-purpose + 1½ teaspoons baking powder + ½ teaspoon salt

Garlic powder: ⅛ teaspoon = 1 average clove

Gingerroot: 1 teaspoon = ¾ teaspoon ground

Grits: 1 cup = 4 cups cooked

Herbs, fresh: 1 tablespoon = 1 teaspoon dried

Lemon: 1 medium = 3 tablespoons juice

Marshmallows: ¼ pound = 16 large; ½ cup = 4 large

Milk, whole: 1 cup = ½ cup evaporated + ½ cup water

Mushrooms: ¼ pound fresh = 1 cup sliced

Mustard, dry: 1 teaspoon = 1 tablespoon prepared

Noodles: 1 pound = 7 cups cooked

Nuts, chopped: ¼ pound = 1 cup

Onion: 1 medium = ¾–1 cup chopped = 2 tablespoons dried chopped (flakes)

Orange: 3–4 medium = 1 cup juice

Pecans: 1 pound shelled = 4 cups

Potatoes: 1 pound = 3 medium

Rice: 1 cup = 3 cups cooked

Spaghetti: 1 pound uncooked = 5 cups cooked

Spinach, fresh: 2 cups chopped = 1 (10-ounce) package frozen chopped

Sugar, brown: 1 pound = 2½ cups

Sugar, powdered: 1 pound = 3½ cups

Sugar, white: 1 pound = 2¼ cups

Vanilla wafers: 22 = 1 cup fine crumbs

SUBSTITUTIONS:

1 slice cooked bacon = 1 tablespoon bacon bits

1 cup buttermilk = 1 cup plain yogurt; or 1 tablespoon lemon juice or vinegar + plain milk to make 1 cup

1 cup sifted cake flour = ⅞ cup sifted all-purpose flour

1 ounce unsweetened chocolate = 3 tablespoons cocoa + 1 tablespoon butter or margarine

1 ounce semisweet chocolate = 3 tablespoons cocoa + 1 tablespoon butter or margarine + 3 tablespoons sugar

1 tablespoon cornstarch = 2 tablespoons flour (for thickening)

1 cup heavy cream (for cooking, not whipping) = ⅓ cup butter + ¾ cup milk

1 cup sour cream = ⅓ cup milk + ⅓ cup butter; or 1 cup plain yogurt

1 cup tartar sauce = 6 tablespoons mayonnaise or salad dressing + 2 tablespoons pickle relish

1 cup tomato juice = ½ cup tomato sauce + ½ cup water

1 cup vegetable oil = ½ pound (2 sticks) butter

1 cup whipping cream, whipped = 6–8 ounces Cool Whip

1 cup whole milk = ½ cup evaporated milk + ½ cup water

MEASUREMENTS:

3 teaspoons = 1 tablespoon

1 tablespoon = ½ fluid ounce

2 tablespoons = ⅛ cup

3 tablespoons = 1 jigger

4 tablespoons = ¼ cup

8 tablespoons = ½ cup or 4 ounces

12 tablespoons = ¾ cup

16 tablespoons = 1 cup or 8 ounces

⅜ cup = ¼ cup + 2 tablespoons

⅝ cup = ½ cup + 2 tablespoons

⅞ cup = ¾ cup + 2 tablespoons

½ cup = 4 fluid ounces

1 cup = ½ pint or 8 fluid ounces

2 cups = 1 pint or 16 fluid ounces

1 pint, liquid = 2 cups or 16 fluid ounces

1 quart, liquid = 2 pints or 4 cups

1 gallon, liquid = 4 quarts or 8 pints or 16 cups

OVEN-TO-CROCKPOT CONVERSIONS:

15–30 minutes in the oven = 1½–2½ hours on HIGH or 4–6 hours on LOW

35–45 minutes in the oven = 2–3 hours on HIGH or 6–8 hours on LOW

50 minutes–3 hours in the oven = 4–5 hours on HIGH or 8–10 hours on LOW

Index

1983
Cellular

The development of commercial cellular systems did not occur rapidly—almost 36 years passed between the initial concept in 1947, and the first commercial systems in 1983. Delays due to regulatory discussions allowed developers to incorporate supporting technologies like microprocessors and integrated circuits into the cellular telephone as we know it. "Cellular" began as a term for analog service transferred from cell to cell, but now refers to all wireless phone services. Statistically, there were one million subscribers by 1987, increasing 1,000% by 1991 with both analog and digital capability. In 2008, there were more than 270 million wireless customers, who used more than 7.7 billion minutes per day.

Text messaging services appeared in 1993. Although "texting" started out slowly, it is now the most widely used and reliable mobile data service, with more than 3.5 billion text messages being sent out daily.

Index

A

B

Index

Index

Index

Index

Index

Index

Q

R

Index

Index

Also Available!

North Texas AT&T Pioneers Cookbook

Best of the Best from Texas Pride Cookbook

Selected Recipes from the Classic North Texas AT&T Pioneer Cookbooks

Texas, with its vastness in size, has two telephone pioneer associations, each of which has published popular cookbooks over the years. These two new Best of the Best Texas editions continue the tradition of the Series with over 350 recipes (in each cookbook) that capture the special flavors of Texas with easy-to-prepare tasteful recipes.

ISBN: 978-1-934193-45-7
6x9 • Comb-bound • 272 pages • Index • $16.95

More Best of the Best Pioneer Cookbooks

6x9 • Comb-bound• 288 pages • Index • $16.95

Bell's Best, *Calling All Cooks*, and *Dogwood Delights* represent the Best of the Best recipes from all the cookbooks that these telephone pioneer associations have published. Each of the cookbooks shown below contains approximately 400 of the most exceptional recipes to be found anywhere.

Mississippi

Best of the Best from Bell's Best Cookbook

ISBN: 978-1-893062-93-1

Alabama

Best of the Best from Calling All Cooks Cookbook

ISBN: 978-1-934193-21-1

Georgia

Best of the Best from Dogwood Delights Cookbook

ISBN: 978-1-934193-39-6

QUAIL RIDGE PRESS
P. O. Box 123 • Brandon, MS 39043 • 1-800-343-1583
E-mail: info@quailridge.com • www.quailridge.com

BEST OF THE BEST STATE COOKBOOK SERIES

ALABAMA
ALASKA
ARIZONA
ARKANSAS
BIG SKY
Includes Montana, Wyoming
CALIFORNIA
COLORADO
FLORIDA
GEORGIA
GREAT PLAINS
Includes North Dakota, South Dakota, Nebraska, and Kansas
HAWAII
IDAHO
ILLINOIS
INDIANA
IOWA
KENTUCKY
LOUISIANA
LOUISIANA II
MICHIGAN
MID-ATLANTIC
Includes Maryland, Delaware, New Jersey, and Washington, D.C.
MINNESOTA
MISSISSIPPI
MISSOURI
NEVADA
NEW ENGLAND
Includes Rhode Island, Connecticut, Massachusetts, Vermont, New Hampshire, and Maine
NEW MEXICO
NEW YORK
NO. CAROLINA
OHIO
OKLAHOMA
OREGON
PENNSYLVANIA
SO. CAROLINA
TENNESSEE
TEXAS
TEXAS II
UTAH
VIRGINIA
VIRGINIA II
WASHINGTON
WEST VIRGINIA
WISCONSIN

All Best of the Best Cookbooks are 6x9 inches, are comb-bound, contain approximately 400 recipes, and total 264–352 pages. Each contains illustrations, photographs, an index, and a list of contributing cookbooks, a special feature that cookbook collectors enjoy. Scattered throughout the cookbooks are short quips that provide interesting information about each state, including historical facts and major attractions along with amusing trivia. Retail price per copy $16.95.

To order by credit card, call toll-free **1-800-343-1583**, visit **www.quailridge.com**, or use the Order Form below.

Order Form

Send check, money order, or credit card info to:
QUAIL RIDGE PRESS • P. O. Box 123 • Brandon, MS 39043

Name ____________________

Address ____________________

City ____________________

State/Zip ____________________

Phone # ____________________

Email Address ____________________

❑ Check enclosed

Charge to: ❑ Visa ❑ MC ❑ AmEx ❑ Disc

Card # ____________________

Expiration Date ____________________

Signature ____________________

Qty.	Title of Book (State) or HOF set	Total

Subtotal ________

Mississippi residents add 7% sales tax ________

Postage ($4.00 any number of books) + $4.00

TOTAL ________